Edward Henry Palmer

The Desert of the Exodus

Journeys on Foot in the Wilderness of the Forty Years' Wanderings

Edward Henry Palmer

The Desert of the Exodus
Journeys on Foot in the Wilderness of the Forty Years' Wanderings

ISBN/EAN: 9783744753487

Printed in Europe, USA, Canada, Australia, Japan

Cover: Foto ©Andreas Hilbeck / pixelio.de

More available books at **www.hansebooks.com**

THE DESERT OF THE EXODUS.

Cambridge:
PRINTED BY C. J. CLAY, M.A.
AT THE UNIVERSITY PRESS.

THE

DESERT OF THE EXODUS

JOURNEYS ON FOOT IN THE WILDERNESS OF THE FORTY YEARS' WANDERINGS

UNDERTAKEN IN CONNEXION WITH THE ORDNANCE SURVEY OF SINAI
AND THE PALESTINE EXPLORATION FUND,

BY

E. H. PALMER, M.A.

FELLOW OF ST JOHN'S COLLEGE, CAMBRIDGE.

WITH MAPS AND NUMEROUS ILLUSTRATIONS FROM PHOTOGRAPHS AND DRAWINGS TAKEN ON THE SPOT BY THE SINAI SURVEY EXPEDITION, AND C. F. TYRWHITT DRAKE.

PART I.

Cambridge:
DEIGHTON, BELL, AND CO.
LONDON: BELL AND DALDY.
1871.

PREFACE.

MANY travellers have crossed the desert to the Holy Land, but no one has hitherto attempted a complete exploration of the Desert of the Exodus, so as to give an exhaustive account of the scenes of Israel's Wanderings. The notices which we have of the Wilderness south of Palestine are so scattered and partial as to be of little service in determining the Scriptural topography of these regions.

Having accompanied the Ordnance Survey Expedition to the Peninsula of Sinai in 1868-1869, and subsequently visited Et Tîh, Idumæa and Moab on behalf of the Palestine Exploration Fund in 1869-1870, I have wandered over a greater portion of this extensive desert than had been ever previously explored. The results of these journeys, performed entirely on foot and extending over a period of eleven months, I now lay before the reader.

Familiarity with the Arabic language, and the privilege of accompanying experienced explorers and scientific men, have given me exceptional advantages, and ensured an accuracy which I could not otherwise have hoped to attain. I have in every case recorded the impressions received upon the spot, and have carefully avoided all theories except such as were actually forced upon me by facts and were, moreover, substantiated by collateral evidence.

I take the opportunity of expressing my deep sense of gratitude for the kind assistance and co-operation which I have received in preparing this volume for the press.

The maps and photographs of the Sinai Survey are reproduced by the kind permission of Major-General Sir Henry James, F.R.S., Director-General of the Ordnance Survey; and the maps of the Negeb and of Moab by permission of the Committee of the Palestine Exploration Fund.

Captain H. S. Palmer, R.E., and the Rev. T. G. Bonney, B.D., Fellow and Tutor of St John's College, Cambridge, have also rendered me the greatest assistance, not only in revising the proof sheets, but in furnishing me with most valuable suggestions on many important points.

The accounts of the Survey and the Physical Geography of Sinai, and of the Egyptian Hieroglyphic

Tablets at Magháráh and Sarábít el Khádim, are derived almost entirely from manuscript notes kindly placed at my disposal by Captain H. S. Palmer, R.E., and Dr S. Birch of the British Museum.

E. H. PALMER.

St John's College, Cambridge,
June, 1871.

CONTENTS.

PART I.

SINAI.

CHAPTER I. THE SINAI SURVEY.

1868—1869.

PAGE

Origin of the Expedition. Reasons for making the survey. Members of the party. Rival claims of Jebels Músa and Serbál. Details of the survey. The Arabs' ideas upon the subject. Nomenclature. Difficulties of the investigation; and method pursued. 1

CHAPTER II. PHYSICAL GEOGRAPHY OF SINAI.

Popular conception of Sinai. General description. The sandstone district; its mineral wealth. The plain of El Gáih. Cretaceous formation. Pertinent nature of Arab nomenclature. Recovery of Scripture names. The granite region 16

CHAPTER III. FROM SUEZ TO SINAI.

Nov. 11—Nov. 21, 1868.

Suez: the start. Our escort. Scenes on loading. Daily camp-life. First night in the desert. 'Ayún Músa. Passage of the Red Sea. 'Ain Hawwárah and Wády Gharandel: probable sites of Marah and Elim. Legend of Abu Zena's horse. Wády Nasb. Sarábít el Khádim: Egyptian remains. Wády Lebweh. Hostilities between the government and the Bedawín. Wády Berráh; "The Speaking Stone." Wády es Sheikh. El Watíyeh: the latter proposed as a site for Rephidim. Tomb and legend of Nebí Sáleh; his probable identity with Moses. A Bedawí greeting. Arrival at Mount Sinai: first impressions. The Rás Sufsáfeh. Reception at the Convent. . 28

CHAPTER IV. THE CONVENT OF MOUNT SINAI.

Foundation and name. Exterior of the Convent. We are introduced to the "brethren." Character of the monks. The Interior; Strangers' apartments; The Mosque; The Church: Chapel of the Burning Bush. The Mount of the Cross. Russian pilgrims. The Library and Archbishop's room. The Refectory. The gardens and Cemetery. Arab servants. Arab traditions relating to the Convent. 56

CHAPTER V. THE BEDAWIN OF SINAI.

Arab life and character. Social relations. Means of livelihood, dress, habits, health, &c. Numbers and origin. Officers and constitution; marriage; love; children; circumcision; burial; religion; sacrifices; festivals; saints; superstitions. 78

CHAPTER VI. MOUNT SINAI.

Nov. 21, 1868—Jan. 1, 1869.

Camp at Jebel Músa. Sálem and the Hyena. Ascent of Mount Sinai. The Pilgrim's Road; Moses' Fount; Chapel of the Œconomos; Legend of Our Lady of the Fleas. The Confessional Archway. Chapel of Elijah; the cypress. Summit of Mount Sinai; the Delivery of the Law. Rás Sufsáfeh and the Plain of Er Ráhah. Continuation of Pilgrims' Road. The Convent of the Forty Martyrs. The Rock in Horeb. The Mould of the Golden Calf. 101

CONTENTS.

CHAPTER VII. THE NEIGHBOURHOOD OF JEBEL MÚSA.

Rocks with legends. Wády T'láh. Bedawín Camp. Storms; a disaster. Collection of Arab stories. Doctoring the Bedawín. Ascent of Jebel Katarína: the Partridge Fountain; view from the summit. 'Abbas Pasha's Palace. Jebel Moneiját. Excursion to Jebel Hadíd. Primeval stone Remains. Maghrabí Treasure-Finders. Wády Nasb. Christmas at Sinai, ... 122

CHAPTER VIII. FROM SINAI TO SERBÁL.

Jan. 1—Jan. 3, 1869.

Striking camp. Er Ráhah and the Nagb Hawa. Supperless halt. Wády Soláf; destructive flood. A Bedawí Poet. Feirán. We dismiss our Arabs; amusing scenes in consequence. Sheikh Hassan. Rephidim; the rock in Horeb; battle with the Amalekites; route from Rephidim to Sinai; Jebel Táhúnah. Hermits' cells. . . 146

CHAPTER IX. FEIRÁN.

Jan. 3—Jan 26, 1869.

Burial ground of Sheikh Abu Shebíb. Date-palms and gardens. El Maharrad; ruins of the ancient convent. Monkish tombs. Jebel Serbál. Wády 'Aleyát; treasure-finders again; a storm; Jebel Moneiját; death in the Arab camp. Wády 'Ajeleh. Ascent of Serbál; the summit; beacon-fires; meaning of the name Serbál. Abu 'l Hosein, the Fox. Visit to Sheikh Hassan; a heavy dinner; an Arabian night's entertainment. . . . 165

CHAPTER X. MUKATTEB AND MAGHÁRAH.

Jan. 26—Feb. 13, 1869.

Journey down Wády Feirán. Wády Mukatteb. The Sinaitic Inscriptions; their nature and authorship. Visit from Sheikh Mansúr. Alone in the Wilderness. Wády Igné; Egyptian mines and hieroglyphic tablets. Anecdotes of the Arabs. An outlaw. Major Macdonald's house. An Egyptian military station. Instruments em-

ployed by the miners. "Sinai Photographed." The
"Bat Cave." 189

CHAPTER XI. WANDERINGS IN THE WILDERNESS.

Feb. 13—March 4, 1869.

Desert shore of the Red Sea. Wády Dhaghádeh; A mud
bath. The Plain of el Gá'ah. Wády Sigillíyeh; Beautiful
landscape effects; We explore an unknown gorge; and
take to the water; horror of old Sálem. Another desert
walk. The Mirage. Abu Suweirah. Jebel Nágús;
curious acoustic phenomenon: legend of the origin of the
sound. Moses' Hot Bath. Excavated chapels. The
village of Tor. Wády Hebrán. More primeval dwellings. Head of Wády Sigillíyeh. Ruined Convents. Wády
Feirán. An Arab strike. 207

CHAPTER XII. THE HIGHWAYS AND BYWAYS OF SINAI.

March 4—March 23, 1869.

Return to Mukatteb and Maghárah. Wády Sidrí. Sarábít
el Khádim. Egyptian remains; their origin and purport;
mines. Wády Nasb. Wády Babá; plague of insects.
Plain of el Markhá. Abu Zenímeh. Wády Taiyebeh;
encampment by the sea. Wádies Ethál and Useit.
Hammám Far'ún; hot springs; legend of Pharaoh's bath;
a hurricane. Jebel Músa again. 229

CHAPTER XIII. THE OUTLYING DISTRICTS OF SINAI.

March 23—April 24, 1869.

Ascent of Umm Shomer: view from the summit; legend of
the Maiden's Rock; mysterious sounds on the mountain.
The science of Gaiyáfeh. The plain of Sened and Jebel
Umm 'Alawí. Copper mines at Jebel Habashí. Trip to
'Ain Hudherah: Erweis el Ebeirig; remains of an Israelitish camp; Kibroth-Hattaavah. Hazeroth. Tomb of
Nebi Sáleh; ceremonies observed there. Rujeim Zuweidíyeh. Preparations for departure. Wády Tarfah. Night
march across el Gá'ah. Homeward bound. . . 246

CHAPTER XIV. THE RESULTS OF THE SINAI EXPEDITION.

Bearings upon the history of the Exodus. Authority for identifying the country surveyed with the Sinai of the Bible. Route of the Israelites from Egypt to Sinai. *Résumé* of Arguments. Conclusion. 269

PART II.

THE FORTY YEARS' WANDERINGS.

CHAPTER I. THE DESERT AND ITS INHABITANTS.

1869—1870.

Return to the East. General description; The Tíh; The "Negeb" or South Country. The Teyáhah Bedawín; their character; mode of life; plundering excursions. Other Arab tribes. Agriculture as a means of civilising the Bedawín. 283

CHAPTER II. THE SOUTHERN EDGE OF THE TÍH.

Dec. 16, 1869—*Jan.* 17, 1870.

Start from Suez; our dress and equipment. Scene on landing. Wády 'Amárah and Bir Abu Suweira. Head of Wády Gharandel. Arab version of the story of *Shylock*. Wády Wutáh. Another Christmas Day in the Desert. We appear in the character of Snake-charmers. Journey from the Convent to 'Ain Hudherah. Jebel 'Arádeh. The Haiwátt Arabs. Wády el 'Ain. 'Ain el 'Elyá; *nawámis*. El Migráh. Wády el Biyar. More primeval remains; arrangement of ancient pastoral camps. Jebel el 'Ejmeh. We enter the Tíh; first impressions. Meeting with a family of Teyáhah Arabs. . . . 301

CHAPTER III. BÁDIET ET TÍH.

Jan. 17—*Feb.* 2, 1870.

Arrival at Nakhl; reception by the Governor; bargaining with the Teyáhah; signing the contract. We start for the scene of our explorations. Our escort. Wády el 'Aggáb; more stone remains. Wády el 'Arísh. Wády Fahdí. Arab battle-field. A Bedawí ballad. Contellet Garaiyeh; remains of an ancient fort. Ascent of Jebel 'Araif. Wády Ma'yín. Wády Lussán; ancient road and remains; Lussán identical with the Roman station of Lysa. 327

CHAPTER IV. THE WILDERNESS OF KADESH.

Feb. 2—*Feb.* 10, 1870.

'Ain Gadís; reasons for its identification with Kadesh; its situation on the southern border of the Holy Land; ascent of the Spies. Site of Eshkol; Dr Robinson's Kadesh. Wády Muweílih. Christian Hermitages. Nature of Arab tribe-marks. Baal worship. 'Ain Gaseimeh. Entrance into the Negeb or South Country. . . . 349

CHAPTER V. THE CITIES OF THE SOUTH.

Feb. 10—*Feb.* 23, 1870.

Wády Seráin. El Bireín; reception by the Arabs; descriptions of the ruins. Wády Hanein; indications of extensive cultivation; El 'Aujeh; "grape mounds;" ruined church and fort. El Meshrifeh and Sebaita identified with Zephath and Hormah; date of the churches. The Hill Country of the Amorites. Saádí. Rehoboth and Sitnah. Khalasah. Beersheba. Haurá. Wády el Khalíl 359

CHAPTER VI. THE SOUTHERN BORDER OF PALESTINE.

Feb. 23—*March* 29, 1870.

The approach to Palestine. Dátraíyeh. Ed Daharíyeh; modern Horites. Hebron; visit to Sheikh Hamzeh.

CONTENTS. xvii

Jerusalem. We start again for the desert. The Jehalín Arabs. Tell "Arád. El Milh. Journey through the heart of Jebel Rakhmeh and Jebel Magráh. Difficulties with the Arabs; Proclamation of War against us. El 'Abdeh. 393

CHAPTER VII. THE MOUNTAINS OF THE 'AZÁZIMEH.

March 30—April 2, 1870.

Wády Marreh. Rujúm Ahmadí; Arab battle-fields. Legend of Jebel Maderah. Interior of the mountain plateau. Wády Hanjúrat el Gattár. Wády Rámán. Direction of the old Roman road. Identification of Gypsaria. Wády Ghamr. Concluding remarks on the identification of the Negeb of Scripture. . 414

CHAPTER VIII. EDOM.

April 2—April 12, 1870.

The 'Arabah. Physical Geography of Edom; its boundaries, geology, fertility, and inhabitants. Modern Rechabites. Nagb er Rubáí. Ascent of Mount Hor; Aaron's tomb; alarm given by the Arabs; a critical situation. "Taking a rise" out of the Fellahín. The Liyátheneh encampment. Arrangements for the journey to Moab. Petra; description of the monuments; the Sík; the Khazneh, its origin and purport; the amphitheatre; tombs with inscriptions; the western cliffs; 'Aireh; Pharaoh's gardens. Snowed up with the Liyátheneh. . 429

CHAPTER IX. FROM PETRA TO SHIHÁN.

April 12—April 19, 1870.

Packing up. Annoyances from the Fellahín. Wády Beidhá. The 'Ammarín break faith with us. El Beidhá and El Bárid; rock-hewn temples and dwellings. Fulfilment of prophecy. Nagb Nemelah. More quarrels with the 'Ammarín; we are stopped on the high-road. Wády Fiddán. The 'Arabah again. Night-march through the Ghor. Ghor es Sáfí; encampment of the Ghawárineh. A wounded robber. Gasr el Bashárîyeh. Seil Garáhí.

The Dead Sea. The waters of Nimrim. Abu K'tainch; rock-hewn hermitage. Ghor el Mezâri. El Lisân; ruins; El 'Aríl. Bathe in the Dead Sea. Visit from Sheikh Ahmed ibn Tarîf. 448

CHAPTER X. MOAB.

April 20—May 10, 1870.

Description of the Country: Kir-Hareseth; meaning of the term. Nagb Jerrah. Camp of the Beni Hamîdeh. Baal Peor. Search for "Moabite stones." "Lot's wife." Site of the cities of the plain. Shîhán. El Yehúdiyeh. "Solomon's tomb." A council of war. Arab hospitality. Journey through Moab. Wády Mojib, the Arnon. Dibon; the Moabite stone. Umm Rasâs; ruined tower; Arab legend. Wády Wâleh. Ancient sites. Mount Nebo. Antiquarian prospects in Moab. The ford of the Jordan. The Promised Land at last. . 471

CHAPTER XI. THE TOPOGRAPHY OF THE EXODUS.

Canons of Criticism. Route of the Israelites; Sinai to Kadesh; additional reasons for the identification of the latter site with 'Ain Gadís; the eleven days' journey from Horeb; The Wilderness of Paran. The mission of the spies. Defeat by the Amalekites and Canaanites. The forty years' Wanderings; their nature and locality; condition of the Israelites during this period. The encampment at Mount Hor. Defeat by "Arad the Canaanite"; the "way of the spies." The journey to compass Mount Seir; stations to the East of Moab. Defeat of Sihon, king of the Amorites. Encampment in the plains of Moab. The Southern Border of Palestine as defined by Moses. Conclusion. 505

APPENDIX.

A. Passage from Antoninus Martyr. . . . 531
B. Nebi Sáleh. 533
C. The Mohammedan History of the Exodus. . . . 533
D. List of Metropolitan, Archiepiscopal and Episcopal towns in the see of the Holy City of Jerusalem. 550

CONTENTS. xix
PAGE
E. Arabic geographical terms. 555
F. Notes on some rock specimens from Sinai, by the Rev.
T. G. Bonney. 556
INDEX. . . 559

ILLUSTRATIONS.

MAPS.

The Peninsula of Sinai. Ordnance Survey . . 1
Special Survey of Mount Sinai. 101
Special Survey of Jebel Serbâl. 165
Route map of the Negeb or South Country. . . 281
Map of Moab. 471

FULL-PAGE ILLUSTRATIONS.

"Lot's wife" . (C. F. Tyrwhitt-Drake)
                                                                                              Frontispiece.
Sections of Jebel Músa and Jebel Serbâl. (Sinai Survey) . 171
Egyptian Tablet at Maghârah. . . (E. H. Palmer) . 202
Jebel Umm Shomer from Abu Shejer. (C. F. Tyrwhitt-Drake) 247
Ain Huderah. Hazeroth. . . ,, . 260
El 'Aujeh. . . . . (Photograph) . 283
Wády Máyín with distant view of
  the Tîh. . . . (C. F. Tyrwhitt-Drake) 327
Wilderness of Kadesh. . ,, . 349
Cairns at Muweileh. . (Photograph) . 354
Town of Sebaita. Zephath. ,, . 359
Cave at El 'Aujeh. . . ,, . 366
Church at El 'Aujeh. . ,, 369
Ancient Fort at El Meshrifeh. . ,, . 371
Ruined Houses at Sebaita. ,, . 375
Gateway of Tower at Sebaita. . ,, . 375
Gateway at El 'Abdeh. Eboda. ,, . 411

CONTENTS.

Woodcuts.

		PAGE
Rás Sufsáfeh from the Plain. . . (Photograph)		53
Gate of the Convent of St Katharine. . ,, .		58
Group of Sinai Bedawín. . . ,,		79
View from the summit of Sinai. . ,,		108
View from the cleft on Rás Sufsáfeh. ,,		110
The Convent Valley from Jebel Moneijáh. . ,,		136
Summit of Sinai from Jebel ed Deir. . ,,		138
Wády Feirán. . . . ,,		153
View from Jebel Táhúneh. ,,		162
Jebal Serbál. . . . . ,,		170
Wády 'Aleyát from the Watershed. . . ,, .		175
Wády Mukatteb. . . . . ,, .		190
Wády Wutáh. . . (C. F. Tyrwhitt-Drake)		308
Jebel 'Arádeh. . . . . ,,		314
Primeval dwellings in Wády el Biyár. ,,		317
El Biyár. . . . . ,,		319
Kharabát Lussán. . ,,		346
Beersheba. . . . ,,		389
Temple at El Bárid. . . ,,		453
Tower at Umm Rasás. . . ,,		498

1

THE DESERT OF THE EXODUS.

PART I.

SINAI.

CHAPTER I.

THE SINAI SURVEY.

Origin of the Expedition. Reasons for making the survey. Members of the party. Rival claims of Jebels Músa and Serbál. Details of the survey. The Arabs' ideas upon the subject. Nomenclature. Difficulties of the investigation; and method pursued.

THE question proposed by Dean Stanley in his masterly exposition of the connexion between Sacred history and Sacred geography, namely, "Can such a connexion be traced between the scenery, the features, the boundaries, the situation of Sinai and of Palestine on the one hand, and the history of the Israelites on the other?" embodies the whole idea of those who conceived and matured the scheme for making an accurate survey of the Peninsula of Sinai. The circumstances which led to the formation of the Sinai Survey Expedition are well known; it was first projected by the Rev. Pierce Butler, rector of

Ulcombe, Kent, whose melancholy and premature death, when he was upon the eve of starting for a preliminary exploration, seemed at first likely to prove a fatal blow to the undertaking; but, through the energy of those to whom he had confided his plans, they have been carried out on a more complete and exhaustive scale than could have been hoped or anticipated. Sir Henry James, with the sanction of the Government, undertook to direct the survey and to bring to bear upon it all the machinery of the Ordnance Survey Department, and its success was henceforward guaranteed.

The coast line of the Peninsula of Sinai had been already laid down by the officers of the Indian navy sent to prepare a chart of the Red Sea; but no systematic survey of the interior had been hitherto attempted.

The information given by travellers who have merely passed through the country, or visited it for a short time, is necessarily circumscribed within narrow limits, and cannot supply a comprehensive account of the physical features; and as all the books and maps yet published are compiled solely from such sources, they do not afford sufficient data for enabling us to judge of the general fitness of the land for the events recorded in the Sacred Narrative of the Exodus.

The great discrepancies which are found in the various accounts of Sinai and Palestine may be traced to several causes: the erroneous impressions which novel scenes make upon a stranger, and which only long residence can rectify; the absence in too many cases of the special training necessary for forming habits of observation; and last, though not least, a practice of regarding all that concerns these sacred spots through a medium of overstrained religious enthusiasm, and a secret desire to bring every possible and impossible site into the traveller's own route.

Some men, it is true, like Dean Stanley and Dr Robinson, are exceptions to this rule; but the former, with all his wonderful powers of observation, was but a comparatively short time in the country, and the latter, though painstaking and accurate, is not altogether free from a tendency to dogmatic theory.

The Rev. F. W. Holland, an explorer of great practical experience, had visited Sinai on three occasions, and spent many months in the careful examination of its general characteristics; but his researches only led him to the conclusion that an impartial and systematic survey of the Sinaitic Peninsula, by unbiassed and experienced men, was absolutely necessary to enable us to discuss with any degree of certainty the disputed questions of the Exodus.

The objects of the survey then were to identify, if possible, the sites mentioned in the Mosaic narrative; or at least to bring back such geographical and other information as should enable Biblical critics to judge for themselves.

For this purpose, we were instructed to make accurate surveys of the two mountains, Jebel Músa and Jebel Serbál, which have been respectively proposed as the true Sinai; and a more general survey of all the routes by which it was possible for the children of Israel to have approached the heart of the Peninsula.

At the head of the party were Captains Wilson and Palmer, of the Royal Engineers, who, together with four non-commissioned officers of the same Corps, were to execute the survey. The Rev. F. W. Holland, of whose former explorations in the Peninsula I have just spoken, also accompanied us, and by his energy and experience rendered invaluable services to the expedition. The Natural History department was entrusted to Mr Wyatt, and to me was assigned the task of investigating the names and traditions of the country, and of copying and deciphering the inscriptions with which the rocks in many parts of Sinai are covered. As well as gathering stories from the Arabs, I was also charged with the collection of entomological curiosities, and the habits of the natives afforded me every facility for combining the two pursuits!

But, besides demonstrating the general capabilities of the country for the passage and sustenance of the Israelitish hosts, the Sinai Expedition it was expected would settle another most important point, one around which the chief interest of the discussion was concentrated, namely, which was the true Sinai?

Biblical geographers have always been divided upon this point into two parties, one of them contending that Jebel Serbál, the highest mountain in the western group, was the scene of the proclamation of the Law; the other supporting the claims of Jebel Músa, the mountain at the base of which stands the Convent of St Katharine. Both parties appeal to tradition in support of their theory, and I will endeavour to shew to which side this inclines.

Arab tradition has been undoubtedly influenced and in many places supplanted by monkish legend, but there are still abundant traces of an oral native tradition of the events of the Exodus. This is well exemplified in the case of the two mountains, Jebel Músa and Jebel Serbâl. From a careful examination of the evidence on both sides I have myself come to the conclusion that the claims of Serbâl are comparatively modern, and that tradition points to the neighbourhood of that mountain rather as the site of Rephidim than of Sinai, and that the true traditional Sinai is Jebel Músa. To this view I have been led by various considerations. First, the title of the "Mount of God," given to Sinai in the Bible, seems to indicate some mountain well known to Moses as being especially favoured by God, most probably the same mountain which was sanctified in the eyes of the Hebrew lawgiver by his previous conference with the Almighty during his first sojourn in the wilderness*. That such was the tradition in the time of Josephus is clear from his statement that Mount Sinai was regarded with awe "*from the rumour that God dwelt there*†." Now, there are two mountains in the Peninsula which bear the name of Moneijâh, or The Conference; but they are so insig-

---

* Exodus iii, 12 seems to leave no doubt that the Mountain of the Burning Bush and the Mountain of the Law are one and the same: "When thou hast brought forth the people out of Egypt, ye shall serve God upon this mountain."

† Antiq. ii. 12.

nificant, both in size and position, as to render it extremely improbable that either of them was the scene of the law-giving. But Jebel Músa itself, on an old Arabic tablet, which purports to be a translation of the original one placed over the convent-door by the founder, to record the building of the Chapel of the Burning Bush, is called Jebel Moneijáh; and this name, I take it, was originally applied to the mountain now called Jebel Músa, or Moses' Mount; the latter title having been adopted by the monks in preference to the old Arabic name, which was then transferred to the neighbouring hill.

Those writers who assume that Jebel Serbál is the true Sinai maintain their theories by such positive assertions that they have gained for them considerable support amongst Biblical scholars. One argument to which they appeal with great confidence is the prevalence of the "Sinaitic Inscriptions" in the neighbourhood of the mountain; but, as I shall presently shew, this line of reasoning is absurd and preposterous, for the inscriptions in question have nothing whatever to do with the Children of Israel, but belong to comparatively modern, and for the most part Christian, times.

When a large colony of monks settled in the Peninsula, they would of course select a spot where natural advantages were combined with traditional interest, and in founding the episcopal city of Feirán at the base of Jebel Serbál, I believe that they pitched upon the site which native tradition at the time pointed out as Rephidim.

This supposition is confirmed by many circumstances. First, Antoninus Martyr speaks of "a small convent or oratory at Feirán, built upon the spot where Moses stood at the battle of Rephidim*." This has always been supposed to refer to the ruins of an extensive monastic establishment situated upon a slight elevation in the bed of the wády. But neither do the remains answer to the description given by Antoninus Martyr of an "oratorium," nor is the situation sufficiently elevated or commanding to render it probable that this was the position occupied by Moses during the battle. There is however a hill immediately above the spot, with a small ruined chapel on its summit, which exactly corresponds with Antoninus Martyr's description; the position, overlooking a large portion of the surrounding country, is just such an one as we should select for the prophet's stand-point, and every circumstance connected with it tends to confirm the idea that it is the veritable site of Rephidim.

When Feirán became a flourishing episcopal city I can well understand that a rivalry should have existed between the two establishments, here and at Jebel Músa, and have led the monks at Feirán to claim for their own grand mountain the honour of being the true Sinai.

As if to support this theory, we discovered that the orientation of the chapel on the summit had been altered at a later date, and directed towards Serbál itself as the point of adoration.

* See Appendix A.

But when Feirán had perished, and the rival establishment came into undisputed possession of the field, the monks of Jebel Músa began to group around their monastery all the most interesting sites, so as to bring them within easy pilgrim distance; thus it is that we have pointed out to us, in defiance of all geography, the spot where Korah, Dathan and Abiram perished, as well as Rephidim and the rock in Horeb which supplied the thirsty tribes, all within an hour's walk of the Convent of St Katharine.

Even on the supposition that Serbál is the Sinai of the Bible, the interest must be confined to its northern slopes; for, although the southern sides are grand and rugged enough, a single glance at their physical features is sufficient to preclude the idea that they can be in any way connected with the giving of the Law.

Of the two rival mountains, Jebels Músa and Serbál, a special survey was made on a scale of six inches to the mile, representing even the minutest features of their rugged scenery.

Besides these, a more general survey was completed, on a scale of two miles to an inch, including all the principal routes and main geographical features in the western half of the Peninsula. The extent of country thus mapped out covers an area of about 3600 miles, the length of the route sketches being 800 miles. In addition to the actual work of the survey, the geology, archæology, ethnology and natural history of the country were carefully examined, and illustrated by photographs and sketches taken on the spot.

The special surveys were of the most difficult kind; the points selected for trigonometrical observation were necessarily at great heights and at wide distances apart, while the country was so rugged that to get from one to another of these stations was frequently a hard day's work, involving a rough walk and a toilsome climb.

There was, moreover, no wood to be procured, and cairns, instead of poles or flagstaffs, had to be erected on the various points of observation; these required whitewashing, in order to make them sufficiently conspicuous; and one or other of the officers could have been often seen clambering up some precipitous crag, and holding the whitewash pot in his mouth, with the pleasant conviction that a false step might cause him to spill the precious contents, and render his day's labour useless.

It was a very common experience, too, for us to reach the top of a peak in a state of profuse perspiration, and five minutes later to stand there so benumbed with cold that we could scarcely hold a pencil, or manipulate the screws of an instrument. The jolting over the rough, loose boulders which do duty for paths is also very trying, especially in a steep descent; you hop from stone to stone like an animated cricket-ball, until every joint seems dislocated and every sinew strained, while occasionally a piece of rock bounds gracefully away from under your feet, and you come down heavily upon your occiput with a piece of sharp granite in the small of your back.

The Sinai mountaineer, however, incurs but few of the dangers incident to ordinary ascents, a steady head, good wind and stout shoes being sufficient to "vanquish" almost any peak in the country.

Here and there, it is true, some awkward places were met with, as in climbing the great westerly peak of Rás Sufsáfeh, along a narrow ledge of rock with a sheer fall of nearly 2000 feet into the valley beneath; but no real difficulties were encountered during the progress of the survey which a bold dash barefooted, or a hoist up with a tent-rope, would not overcome.

The survey of Serbál was more difficult than that of Jebel Músa. Here, the position of our camp, depending of course on the proximity of water, was not so central; the ascents were much steeper, the heights above camp greater; and, as flaky, crumbling schist in many instances took the place of the hard, firm granite, the walking in the wádies was infinitely more toilsome and fatiguing.

In the low lands and plains, where the features of the country were less rugged and intricate, quicker progress was made. But there, instead of the bracing atmosphere of the mountains, we had to contend against fierce heat and stifling simooms, and the expenditure of vital energy was consequently greater.

The different altitudes* at which we worked

* The heights as determined by the Ordnance Survey are as follows:

	FEET.
Jebel Serbál . . .	6734.
Convent of St Katharine .	5020.
Convent of El Arba'ín .	5624.
Jebel Músa (summit) . .	7359.
Jebel Katharína . . .	8526.

varied from the sea level to some eight thousand feet above it, and the constant changes of temperature to which we were thus exposed would have been extremely trying, had it not been for the hard exercise, clear air and glorious scenery, which gave tone and vigour to both body and mind.

The native Arabs served as guides, and were employed in carrying the heavier instruments when observations were to be made. For the latter work *bedan* (ibex) hunters were generally selected, as they alone are acquainted with the mountain paths and peaks.

The survey was a profound mystery to the Arabs, and at first the cause of no small suspicion. All this writing, they argued, could bode no good to the country: and on more than one occasion we received solemn deputations requesting to be informed whether we were not measuring the Peninsula with a view to purchasing it for the Christians, and ejecting the true believers from their patrimony. When we told them that we had no object but to establish the truth of the history of "our Lord Moses and the Beni Israel," they accepted the explanation outwardly, for politeness' sake, but it was clear from their manner that they entertained no very exalted opinion of the intellectual capacity of those who could think that it required proof at all. Sálem, the chief guide of the expedition, was more experienced, and had accompanied Mr Holland during his previous explorations. He acquiesced in whatever was done, and always lent a willing hand; but at heart he regarded the proceedings with supreme contempt, and drew a very unfavourable comparison between the minute and, to his mind, tedious work of the expedition and the rapid exploits of his former master. "Why," said he to me one day, "the Captáns spend hours and hours on a single mountain, and don't make much of it after all. Now Khawájah Hollol *was* a *jedaʻ* (athlete), and did not waste his time looking through spy-glasses all day; no, he used to take a book in one hand and a pen in the other, and write it all down as he walked along."

My own work consisted chiefly in ascertaining from the Bedawín the correct nomenclature of the Peninsula, and the task was far from easy. Even in our own country, with all the advantage of ancient records and an intelligent population, it is often difficult to determine the correct nomenclature of a single district, but in the desert of Arabia, without civilisation and without records or literature of any kind, the difficulties are greatly increased. The language also has always proved a fertile source of error in previous investigations. The traveller either relies upon the fidelity of his dragoman's interpretation or possesses a sufficient knowledge of Arabic to question the Bedawín for himself. In the first case accuracy is impossible, for the dragoman is both unwilling and unable to prosecute the required investigations. He is generally an illiterate and mercenary being between whom and the Bedawín no sympathy or friendship can exist, and, strange as the assertion may appear, his language even is not theirs.

If on the other hand the traveller has obtained a previous knowledge of Arabic, I am only repeating my own experience when I say that, until he has mixed for some time with the Bedawín, and accustomed his ear to the peculiarities of their dialect, he cannot rely upon a single piece of information that he may have received; and thus it is that the most startling errors have crept into our books and maps. As an instance of this, I may mention the name *Serábit el Khádim*, which is set down in Russegger's map of Sinai as *Serabut petah Khadem*, evidently a dragoman's mistake, as *petah* represents the word *betá'*, which in the vulgar Egyptian dialect is used as a sign of the genitive case.

The Arabs of one locality are totally ignorant of the nomenclature of their neighbours, and cannot understand the motives which induce another person to feel any interest in the subject. Shrewd and intelligent in their own sphere, they are at a loss to comprehend the simplest ideas of civilised life, and this want of a community of thought between the enquirer and respondent is a great stumbling-block in the way of accurate investigation.

The ingenious stupidity of the Bedawín was often very perplexing, as the following instance will shew. During the early part of my stay in Sinai I sought for every opportunity of mastering such expressions and idioms in the Towarah language as differed from those in ordinary use; and not feeling certain as to the particular form of the interrogative particle "when" employed by them, I enquired of an intelligent Arab with whom I chanced to be walking. To make the question as plain as possible, I said, "Supposing you were to meet a man with an ibex on his shoulder, how should you ask him when he shot it?" "I shouldn't ask him at all," he replied, "because I shouldn't care." "But if you did care," I persisted, "what should you say to him?" "What should I say to him? why, I should say good morning!" This was not satisfactory, so we walked on in silence for some minutes, when I suddenly observed, "Sâleh, I saw your wife." "*Mitein?*" said he, startled, "*when?*" and down went the word in my note-book. On another occasion I asked an Arab if he knew why a certain wády was called *Khabár*. "Of course I do," he returned contemptuously, "to distinguish it from other wádies, just as you're called Bundit (Pundit) to distinguish you from Hollol."

Another difficulty that had to be guarded against is indicated by Robinson in his *Biblical Researches*, Vol. I. p. 112. "A tolerably certain method of finding any place at will is to ask an Arab if its name exist. He is sure to answer yes, and to point out some point at hand as its location. In this way, I have no doubt, we might have found a Rephidim, or Marah, or any place we chose."

If more attention were paid to these distinctions and to the character of the people, many errors of travellers and explorers would be avoided. I need not expatiate upon the value of such accuracy both to the Biblical critic and the geographer, for, as the Archbishop of Dublin has truly and pithily remarked,

Arab tradition is "fossilised" in their nomenclature, and often furnishes undying testimony to the truth of Scripture.

The method pursued by me was as follows:

I accompanied the officers during the actual process of making the survey, and taking with me the most intelligent Bedawín that I could find belonging to the particular locality, I asked the name of each place as its position was noted down upon the sketch. I then made further enquiry in the neighbourhood from other Arabs, and never accepted a name without independent and separate testimony to corroborate the information I had at first received. Having in this manner satisfied myself of the accuracy of my information, I proceeded to enquire into the meaning and origin of the names, and set down against each one not only what I knew to be the signification of the word, but the meaning which my informant himself attached to it. I found this method invaluable for testing the accuracy of my orthography; and although the reasons given were not unfrequently trivial or even ridiculous, they served the purpose of corroborative evidence.

With the exception of our first few days' journey from Suez to Jebel Músa, the whole work of the survey was performed on foot, and the result of my own experience in this particular is that I have learnt to consider as one of the greatest miracles of the Exodus the fact that the shoes of the Children of Israel "waxed not old upon their feet."

CHAPTER II.

PHYSICAL GEOGRAPHY OF SINAI.

Popular conception of Sinai. General description. The sandstone district: its mineral wealth. The plain of El Gâah. Cretaceous formation. Pertinent nature of Arab nomenclature. Recovery of Scripture names. The granite region.

THE popular conception of Sinai, even in the present day, seems to be that a single isolated mountain which may be approached from any direction rises conspicuous above a boundless plain of sand. The Bible itself, if read without the light of modern discovery, certainly favours this idea, and the mountainous character of the country is by no means strongly brought out in the Sacred Narrative. Exodus xxxii, 12 is perhaps the only passage in the Pentateuch where "the mountains" of Sinai are spoken of: "Wherefore should the Egyptians speak and say, For mischief did he bring them out to slay them *in the mountains?*" In the account of Elijah's conference with the Almighty on "Horeb, the mount of God" (1 Kings xix, 11) we are told that "a great and strong wind *rent the mountains* and brake in pieces the rocks before the Lord," but, with the exception of these meagre and scattered notices, Mount Sinai is always alluded to in the Bible as though it stood alone and unmistakable in the midst of a level desert plain. Even in those parts which approach most nearly to our conception of what a desert ought to be—a solid ocean bounded only by the horizon or by a barrier of distant hills—sand is the exception, and the soil resembles rather a hard gravel path than a soft and yielding beach.

Sinai is a triangular peninsula situated between the two arms of the Red Sea, the Gulf of Suez and the Gulf of 'Akabah, with the escarpment of the Tíh plateau projecting wedgewise into it from its northern base. The sides of the triangle measure about 190 and 130 miles respectively, and the length of its base is nearly 150 miles: this gives an area of 11,600 square miles; or, approximately, twice that of Yorkshire.

A broad belt of sandstone crosses the Peninsula immediately south of the Tíh frontier and extends nearly from shore to shore. On the west, it commences a little north of Wády Wutáh and reaches as far south as Jebel Mokatteb. The mountains of this district are for the most part low and isolated, with broad plateaux for their summits; but the fantastic shapes and gorgeous colouring of the rocks more than compensate for the deficiency in height; and some of the sandstone peaks, such as Umm Rijlain, are among the most striking features in the Peninsula. Broad undulating plains, and narrow valleys with sheer precipitous sides, are amongst the most conspicuous features of this belt of country. Of the plains the largest is the Debbet er Ramleh, which skirts the base of the Tíh range and occupies about one-eighth of the whole sandstone area.

This formation is rich in mineral wealth, containing many veins of iron, copper and turquoise. The absence of all conveniences for smelting and transport deprives them of commercial value at the present day, but the ancient Egyptians, appear to have had greater facilities and to have worked the ores upon a very extensive scale. The neighbourhood of Serábít el Khádim and Maghárah abounds in mines, in hieroglyphic tablets recording the names and titles of the kings under whose auspices they were worked, and in other archæological relics of the highest interest and antiquity.

South of the sandstone belt is a triangular mass of mountains, its highest peaks reaching to an elevation of between 8000 and 9000 feet, its two sides running nearly parallel with those of the Peninsula itself, and finally meeting them in a common apex at Rás Muhammed. A strip of flat desert bounds this triangle on the east and west sides; on the eastern side it disappears here and there when the mountains come down in sharp escarpments to the sea; on the western side it grows gradually larger as it runs southward and obtains its maximum breadth at Tor. Here it is a broad undulating plain of gravel, which, as the largest unbroken expanse in the country, is called emphatically El Gá'ah, or "*the* plain."

Its monotonous level is only broken by a low range of hills skirting the shore, and by two small conical hills in its centre, which, from their peculiar conformation, the Arabs have appropriately named Gerún 'Utúd, "The budding horns of a kid."

The cretaceous formation skirts the seaboard in a long narrow slip extending southward from Suez to Tor, and bounded on the north-east by the escarpment of the Tíh, on the east and south-east by the sandstone and granite districts. Here and there the shore-plains are interrupted by precipitous bluffs of limestone. This region is the dreariest of all; the mountains, which do not at any point attain an elevation of more than 2600 feet, are colourless and almost featureless, rising at first gently from the shore-plains and then more sharply and abruptly to their highest ridges. Even here one sometimes finds a narrow gorge or picturesque valley, a cool stream rippling along its bed, and caper plants festooning gracefully over its white and dazzling walls. The mountains of this cretaceous district are confined to its southern portion; from Wády Gharandel northwards the country is a smooth and level desert sloping gradually towards the sea.

One of the most striking characteristics of this tract is the endless ramification of small valleys met with in some of its plains and plateaux. This formation is especially well exemplified in the plateau west of Sarbút el Jemel, where a perfect network of little chalky wádies meets the eye, and where in the Arab nomenclature, which always seizes upon the most salient points of the physical geography, one of the principal of these groupings or *quasi* river-systems is called *Shebeikeh*, the "Net."

The Arabs, though without any sense of natural beauty and deficient in the faculty of generalization, are nevertheless acute observers of minor detail; and their nomenclature is singularly pertinent, illustrating in a remarkable manner the physical aspect of the country.

In every locality, each individual object, whether rock, mountain, ravine or valley, has its appropriate name.

This nomenclature is entirely Arab, and very few if any traces of Scriptural names exist; but it is quite possible that some of the present names may suggest a clue to the recovery of the older appellations, for it is a well-known fact that the Arabs are very averse from retaining any name which they themselves cannot understand; and in many parts of Palestine we find the Hebrew words just sufficiently distorted from their original form to give them an intelligible Arabic meaning. In Wády Feirán, for example, there is an evident reminiscence of the ancient name Paran; the Bedawín are unable to pronounce the letter *p*, and the word, becoming Fáran, would soon degenerate with them into *Feirán*, the Valley *of Mice*, a name which would appear particularly applicable to a place where their monkish predecessors had covered the hill-sides with excavated tombs and cells resembling, as the natives say, the burrows of field-mice or jerboas.

The name Horeb also, having no meaning to the Arab ear, has long since perished; but it reappears in Jebel 'Aríbeh, a mountain in the immediate neighbourhood of Jebel Músa, and so called from a plant, 'Aríbeh, with which it abounds.

The grandest mountain features are found amid the crystalline rocks which occupy the central portion of the Peninsula. These consist chiefly of granite, or porphyry, gneiss and mica-schist. The scenery in the granite is far more imposing than in the other formations; in these last, however, the bright and beautiful colouring of the doleritic or dioritic dykes with which the gneissic and schistose rocks are streaked gives a peculiarly pleasing and romantic effect to the landscape.

The granite mountains lie in such a rugged tumbled chaos as scarcely to admit of classification. It has been usual to divide them into three clusters—that in the west having Mount Serbál for its highest point, the central (or Sinai) group of which one of the peaks of Jebel Katharína is the highest in the Peninsula, and the group to the south-east, culminating in the magnificent peak of Umm Shomer.

This division is useful, both because it enables us to retain a comprehensive idea of the leading features of the country, and because to these three the interest of the enquiry is chiefly confined. But there are several other peaks and groups which are scarcely less grand and imposing. In the west, the huge red mass of Jebel el Benát, with its graceful outline, arrests the attention almost as much as Serbál itself, and, in the heart of the Peninsula, Jebel Umm 'Alawí, towering above the magnificent plain which stretches from its north-east slope, did it but lie in the ordinary traveller's path, would long ago have become a claimant for the honour of being the true Mountain of the Law.

The most conspicuous features of the granite region are the long range north of the easternmost Wády Nasb, the high sierra to the south, which, with Jebel eth Thebt for its northern and highest point, reaches almost to Rás Muhammed, and the great granite wall shutting in the central mass of plutonic rocks in the midst of which Mount Sinai lies.

The long winding valleys by which the mountain groups are intersected are called wádies. They are not at all like the valleys to which we are accustomed in Europe, but present rather the appearance of dry, sandy river-beds. They are in fact the courses along which the torrents from the mountains find their way down to the sea; but, as rain seldom falls, and as there is no soil or vegetation on the mountain sides to collect or absorb the gentler showers when they do come, the valleys are never filled except on the occasion of some fierce storm bursting over the mountains which they drain. Seldom as this event occurs, and partial as it always is, the waterworn appearance of the shelving sides of the wádies, and the large boulders of rock which lie scattered about their beds, shew that at some time or other nearly every one of them has been the scene of one of these terrible *seils* or floods. The rainfall in the country, though scanty, is sufficient to replenish the few springs and rivulets which form the permanent water-supply. So rapid is the evaporation, that a few minutes after a shower has fallen the surface of the ground is as dry and thirsty looking as before, but a large proportion must be absorbed and retained in the gravel with which the wády beds are filled; the great floods also, which occasionally rush so impetuously down to the sea, must yet leave much moisture behind.

Although the general aspect of the country is one of sheer desolation and barrenness, it must not be supposed that there is no fertility to be found there. There are no rivers, yet many a pleasant little rivulet fringed with verdure may be met with here and there, especially in the romantic glens of the granite district. At Wádies Nasb and Gharandel are perennial, though not continuous, streams and large tracts of vegetation. At that part of Wády Feirán where the valley contracts in breadth and concentrates the moisture, we find the most considerable oasis in the Peninsula; and behind the little sea-port of Tor, also, where a depression in the great alluvial plain of El Gá'ah collects the moisture, there exists a large and magnificent grove of date-palms.

Besides these, the more fertile spots produce thorns, acacia, tamarisk, sidr and other trees, while most of the valleys contain some vegetation; in the highlands, myrrh, thyme and other fragrant herbs, and in the plains, *retem* or broom (the juniper-tree of Scripture), *sekkerán* (a kind of mallow), *'abeithirán* and countless plants on which the camels feed. Even the barest and most stony hill-side is seldom entirely destitute of vegetation; and the Jericho rose, an extraordinary bibulous plant, which has the faculty of expanding when placed in water after lying in a cabinet for years, may be seen on the most unpromising spots.

The herbage in the valleys is of a pale sickly green, and in the summer season often so burnt up that it crumbles to powder at the slightest touch; but the first shower of spring recalls the plant into life, and, like the rod of Aaron, the dry and withered sticks again "bring forth buds and bloom blossoms." (Numbers xvii. 8.) No visible effect however is produced by all this vegetation upon the general desert aspect of the country: to Moses and the Children of Israel three thousand years ago Sinai must have looked precisely as it does at the present day.

Many of the less frequented wâdies too, especially those which run down from the great granite clusters of mountains, are watered by pleasant streams, and teem with natural vegetation. The old monkish colonists of the place availed themselves extensively of the advantages afforded by these spots to plant gardens and olive-groves, many of which remain to the present day. These gardens, so long as they were tended with care and skill, acted as so many sponges, or dams, to stay the course of the torrents, and, by holding and husbanding the water, turned the terrible agent of destruction into a blessing and a boon. This leads to the consideration of another most important question, namely, Was the country more fertile in the time of the Exodus than it is now? While admitting the miraculous manner in which the twelve tribes were supported, we shall disarm many objectors if we can shew with reason that there were resources in the country of which they might have availed themselves at certain seasons and at certain places, since this would account for the silence of the Bible upon many points which would otherwise seem inexplicable—I mean in cases where no special miraculous provision is recorded.

That rain actually fell during the passage of the Israelites through the country we learn from Psalm lxviii. 7—9; "O God, when thou wentest forth before the people, when thou didst march through the wilderness; Selah. The earth shook, *the heavens also dropped* at the presence of God; even Sinai itself was moved at the presence of God, the God of Israel. *Thou, O God, didst send a plentiful rain*, whereby thou didst confirm thine inheritance, when it was weary." And such passages as "the clouds poured out water," Psalm lxxvii. 17, where the allusion is evidently to Sinai, also tend to confirm the supposition that the Peninsula was better supplied with water at the time of the Exodus.

There are still many groves of acacia and other trees in the Peninsula, and these, like the gardens, form a sort of barricade against the force of the torrents. Now when one of them is destroyed, and a storm comes, whatever vegetation depended on or was protected by the forest is soon swept away, and barrenness and devastation mark the course of the stream down to the sea. It is a well-known fact that rain falls more gently and regularly where there is vegetation. Now the Bible tells us that there existed a large population in and near Sinai at the time of the Exodus, and the traces of them which still remain indicate that they, like the old monks, did husband to the utmost the resources of the country.

Again, there are abundant vestiges of large colonies of Egyptian miners, whose slag heaps and smelting furnaces are yet to be seen in many parts of the Peninsula. These must have destroyed many miles of forest in order to procure the fuel necessary for carrying on their operations; nay, more, the children of Israel could not have passed through without consuming vast quantities of fuel too. But, if forest after forest disappeared in this way, if population dwindled down to a few non-agricultural tribes, and cultivation were neglected, then the rain that falls so seldom would no longer stay to fertilize the land, but in an unimpeded torrent would find its way down to the sea; a burning summer sun would soon complete the work, and a few ages would make the Peninsula of Sinai what we see it now. I do not think it necessary to reason away the signal miracles by which the Jewish hosts were fed, but I do believe that whatever God thought fit, that He did for His chosen people, and that God's servant, Nature, did the rest.

The present sterility of the country makes the

vicissitudes of climate much more severe in Sinai than in other parts of Arabia. You have the extremes of heat and cold, frequently a difference of fifty degrees between the temperature of night and day, and there is little or no fuel to counteract the one, or shade to repel the other.

The very nakedness of the rocks imparts to the scene a grandeur and beauty peculiarly its own. For, as there is no vegetation to soften down the rugged outlines of the mountains or conceal the nature of their formation, each rock stands out with its own distinctive shape and colour as clearly as in some gigantic geological model map. In some wádies the mountain sides are striped with innumerable veins of the most brilliant hue, thus producing an effect of colour and fantastic design which it is impossible to describe. These effects are heightened by the peculiar clearness of the atmosphere and the dazzling brightness of the sunlight; one part of a mountain will glow with a ruddy or golden hue, while the rest is plunged in deepest shade. Sometimes a distant peak will seem to blend with the liquid azure of the sky, while another stands out in all the beauty of purple or violet tints; and, with what would seem the mere skeleton of a landscape, as beautiful effects are produced as if the bare rocks were clad with forests and vineyards or capped with perpetual snows. Nature, in short, seems here to shew that in her most barren and uninviting moods she can be exquisitely beautiful still.

CHAPTER III.

FROM SUEZ TO SINAI.

Suez: the start. Our escort. Scenes on loading. Daily camp-life. First night in the desert. 'Aiyún Músá. Passage of the Red Sea. 'Ain Hawwárah and Wády Gharandel: probable sites of Marah and Elim. Legend of Abu Zena's horse. Wády Nasb. Sarábít el Khádim: Egyptian remains. Wády Lebweh. Hostilities between the government and the Bedawín. Wády Berráh; "The Speaking Stone." Wády es Sheikh. El Watíyeh: the latter proposed as a site for Rephidim. Tomb and legend of Nebí Sáleh: his probable identity with Moses. A Bedawí greeting. Arrival at Mount Sinai: first impressions. The Rás Sufsáfeh. Reception at the Convent.

HAVING thus given a general account of the nature of our work and of the physical aspect of the country itself, I now come to the more personal experiences of the Expedition, the actual narrative of our wanderings in the wilderness.

On the 8th of November, 1868, I received a telegram informing me that my future companions had arrived at Suez; and, packing up with all speed, I made my way to the Cairo railway station. It was early morning, and from every minaret rung the clear voice of the Muezzin warning the hushed city that "prayer is better than sleep;" and the subdued blue light which fell upon the hundred domes of Cairo threw into deeper shade the goblin forms of the prickly pear-trees that bordered the path. A few hours more and I had reached my destination, and beheld Egyptian village-life in all its squalid opthalmic reality. Yet the half-blind dirty creatures seemed happy, and I came to the conclusion that good spirits and bad living are not incompatible after all. A noisy crowd, dressed in every variety of costume which we are accustomed to associate with dramatic pictures of Blue Beard (1*d*. plain, 2*d*. coloured) awaited the arrival of the train, and a dozen sturdy Muslims at once began a contest for the possession of my baggage. As I did not interfere, they followed me to the Hotel in a sort of funeral procession, with four bearers to each of my two modest portmanteaus, my umbrella as chief mourner bringing up the rear. For all this pomp I disbursed a *sebáin*, not quite threepence.

The Viceroy of Egypt had given orders that our baggage should be passed unopened through the Custom-house, and that every assistance should be given us by the officials. The Peninsular and Oriental Company kindly allowed us to purchase provisions from their stores, and as Mr Holland had sent on word to his old friends amongst the Towarah Bedawín to meet us with camels at Suez, we were soon able to arrange all the preliminaries for a start. Three days sufficed to provide water-skins, barrels and the other numerous requisites for desert travel; and on the 11th of November we crossed over the head of the Gulf of Suez with no further catastrophe than a fight between the rival boatmen who carried our stores. Owing, however, to the awkward construction of the pier, and the obstinate ill-temper of a Barbary negro who had charge thereof, we did not accomplish our landing until sunset was drawing near, and the tents were accordingly pitched by the sea-shore. The harbour of Suez presented a very gay appearance, the ships being all illuminated in honour of the arrival of a new German consul. The young moon shed a soft and timid radiance over the scene, as if ashamed to burst too rudely through the veil of night, when, with the dark mysterious desert stretching far away behind me, I lay down to sleep for the first time in a tent.

On the following morning we bade adieu to civilisation. I shall not easily forget the impressions with which I entered the desert. I had been for years familiar with the literature of Arabia, and had read with a certain vague interest the descriptions of desert life; but here it was at last in all its reality before me.

It was not without considerable misgivings, too, that I essayed to mount a camel for the first time. The camel is a much over-rated beast, and is the very incarnation of peevish ill-temper. Docile he is, but apparently from no other reason than sheer stupidity. No sooner do you approach him than he sets up a hideous snarling groan; the driver pulls his head forcibly down to the ground, and you seize the opportunity of jumping on to his back. But before you can secure your seat, you are suddenly pitched violently forward, then as violently backwards; for the creature gets up by jerks, and only half of him at a time. When once mounted, the motion is not so unpleasant as it has been described, and a very few days makes you quite at home in your elevated seat.

Our train consisted of forty-two camels, under the conduct of two sheikhs, 'Eid and Mansúr, for the Towarah are so poor that no single sheikh was able to supply the whole number. 'Eid was a tall, thin, and active old man; his face was handsome, though not quite of the true Bedawí type, but when at rest it was decidedly classic and severe. In reality, however, he was a childish old booby, for all his heroic looks, and had no control whatever over his men. He was constantly skipping about like a marionette, and screaming out orders which nobody minded in the least. On such occasions his face would assume an agonized expression, his mouth would stretch from ear to ear, and he would shout, or rather yell, '*Ta'áloo yá ooláá!*'—"Come, oh, children!"—in the wildest and most ludicrous manner. The "children" apostrophized would smoke their pipes the while with placid indifference, leaving poor old 'Eid to do all the work himself. Mansúr was a man with rather more determination of character, and, but for rheumatism, would have been a serviceable ally. As to personal appearance, he might have sat for a portrait of the patriarch Abraham himself*.

The task of apportioning the loads is always a difficult one; the Arabs scream, swear, and struggle as though about to engage in a sanguinary fight; and each one, as he gets the opportunity, will seize upon the lightest things which he can find, and, if not immediately repressed, will hasten off to his camel with about a quarter of his proper load, leaving his comrades to fight over the heavier burdens.

One morning, before the camels were loaded, a rather amusing quarrel occurred between our two sheikhs respecting a dromedary that still remained unemployed. The presence of Holland and myself soon put an end to the strife; but 'Eid, having once let his "angry passions rise," could not immediately suppress his agitation. For some moments he executed an extemporary "breakdown," expressive of indignation and defiance, and then suddenly catching sight of his own son Embárak, who had remained a passive spectator of the scene, he seized a camel rope, and thrashed that unoffending youth in a manner as energetic as it was vague. After this, he set about his work with an air of great relief.

There is but little variety in camp-life in the desert, and a description of one day's journey may answer for all the rest. At sunrise every one is

---

* Since writing the above I have again visited Sinai, and find that poor old Mansúr is dead.

astir; a simple toilette, a still more simple meal, and you pack up your things in preparation for the start. Then comes a repetition of the noise and clamour incident on loading, you mount your dromedary, and, when once fairly under weigh, the whole caravan trails noiselessly along the sand. Following the path marked out by the skeletons of camels which lie bleaching in the sun, you ride on until the noonday heat and glare compel you to seek a little rest beneath some friendly shade, if there is any to be had, though very frequently you must put up with such shelter as a white umbrella, or the unsavoury vicinity of a kneeling camel can afford. In England one knows nothing of the luxury of shade, and cannot appreciate what it really means. How often, when reclining, five of us, beneath a dried-up furze-bush no bigger than a good-sized geranium, have we consumed our lunch of dates and biscuits, washed down with just one drink of lukewarm water beautifully flavoured with goat-skin, and envied the happy terrier that laps the cool puddle of his native land!

After lunch the march is resumed until sunset, and then commences the really enjoyable part of the day. The tents are pitched, and dinner is prepared. The Arabs settle themselves cosily round the camp-fires to prepare their evening meal, and for an hour or so before retiring for the night comfort and repose reign around. The first night in the desert was an era in my life; it seemed as if all the vague images of my early dreams were about to assume a life-like reality which they had never worn for me till then. A fresh breeze blew into the tent, causing no apprehensions of nightly chills, but infusing new vigour into both body and mind. The flickering camp-fires shed a lurid glow over the little knots of swarthy Bedawín as they reposed after the fatigues of the day, and produced a wondrously picturesque and Rembrandt-like effect. The hushed tones of those who had not yet fallen asleep, the whirring of a hand-mill here and there, the half-plaintive, half-surly groaning of the camels—these were the only sounds which disturbed the stillness of the night. I contemplated the scene around me with mingled feelings of delight and awe. I was reclining perchance upon the very spot where the Children of Israel had encamped when fleeing from their Egyptian persecutors, and I could not help comparing my situation to some extent with theirs. I had just left the noisy bustling crowd of Cairo's streets, and had escaped into the freedom of the great lone wilderness, and I too felt that sense of special Divine protection which must have been present to them, for never so much as in the desert does one feel that God is nigh. He it is that enables man to pass in safety through this dreary waste, and whether it be by direct miraculous intervention, as in the case of the Chosen People, or by the scarcely less wonderful agency of reason and foresight, still it is His hand alone that guides him on.

Two hours' ride from Suez brought us to 'Ayún Músa, or Moses' Wells, a beautiful little oasis in the desert. It consists of a few springs of limpid but brackish water, small pools with gardens of palms and tamarisks around them, as well as beds of vegetables and culinary herbs. These gardens are kept by a Frenchman and some Arabs, who have provided summer-houses for the convenience of those who resort thither from Suez to enjoy the fresh desert air. They form the market-gardens from which the vegetable supply of Suez is principally drawn. There exists also a solitary pool upon the top of a neighbouring hill of sand, having one single palm beside it. The beautiful view which this spot commands more than makes up for the absence of vegetation; to the north stretches a vast level plain of sand, with a long chain of mountains bordering it on the east; and on the north-west the bold promontory of Rás Atákah overhangs the Gulf, its noble outlines and lovely purple tints, clearly seen against the azure sky, presenting a scene at once picturesque and grand.

Here tradition places the site of the Passage of the Red Sea; and certain it is that, at least within the range over which the eye can wander, the waters must have closed in upon Pharaoh's struggling hosts. The miracle of the Passage of the Red Sea is so important in its bearings upon the whole question of the Exodus that many and various opinions have been advanced both as to its site and character. The obvious route of the Israelites from Egypt would have been by the ordinary road to Palestine through the Philistine territory; but we are expressly told that "God led them not through the way of the land of the Philistines, although that was near; for God said, Lest peradventure the people repent when they see war, and they return to Egypt; But God led the people about, through the way of the wilderness of the Red Sea." (Ex. xiii. 17, 18.) Now this "way of the wilderness" must also have passed round the head of the Gulf, and the two routes must have been at this point coincident.

From the narrative in Exodus xiv. it would seem that the Egyptians came upon them before they had rounded the head of the Gulf, so as to compel them either to take to the water or fall into their enemies' hands, equally fatal alternatives, from which nothing but a miracle, such as that recorded, could have saved them. But natural agencies, miraculously accelerated, are mentioned as the means employed by God in working out this signal deliverance, and we need not therefore suppose anything so contrary to the laws of nature as that the children of Israel crossed between two vertical walls of water in the midst of the deep sea, according to the popular mode of depicting the scene. Some writers have imagined that a great change has taken place in the level of the sea since the time of the Exodus, but recent examination does not at all confirm this hypothesis, while there is abundant evidence that the northern end of the Gulf of Suez has been gradually silted up, and that in consequence the shore-line has steadily advanced further and further southwards. It follows from this that, if, according to the view held by many modern authorities, the Passage took place at the head of the Gulf as it existed at the time of the Exodus, the Israelites must have crossed at a point several miles north of its present limits. Then we are told that "the Lord caused the sea to go back by a strong east wind all that night, and made the sea dry land, and the waters were divided." This is no sudden division of the waters involving a suspension of physical laws, though to my mind it is much more wonderful as showing how those laws were subservient to the Divine purpose and will. A strong wind blowing from the East at the moment of the setting in of the ebb tide might so drive back the waters that towards the sea they would be some feet higher than on the shore side. Such a phenomenon is frequently observed in lakes and inland seas, and if there were, as there would very likely be at the head of the Gulf, any inequality in the bed of the sea or any chain of sand-banks dividing the upper part of the Gulf into two basins, that portion might be blown dry and a path very soon be left with water on either side. As the parting of the sea was caused by an East wind, the sudden veering of this wind to the opposite quarter at the moment of the return tide would bring the waters back with unusual rapidity. This seems to have been actually the case, for we find that the waters returned, not with a sudden rush overwhelming the Egyptians at once, but gradually and at first, as we might expect, saturating the sand so that "it took off their chariot-wheels that they drave them heavily."

In the hurricane and darkness of the night this would naturally cause such a panic and confusion as to seriously retard them in their passage; but in the mean time the waters were too surely advancing upon them, and when morning broke "Israel saw the Egyptians dead upon the sea-shore." The verse last quoted seems to show conclusively that the wind did veer round to the west, for otherwise, with the East wind still blowing the corpses of Pharaoh and his host would have been driven away from the Israelites and thrown up upon the opposite shore.

The exact spot at which the miracle took place must always remain a matter of mere speculation, but there can be little doubt that at this point, 'Ayún Músa, (Moses' Wells) we are upon the track of the Israelites at the commencement of their desert journey. In the Bible narrative, immediately after the account of the destruction of the Egyptian army and of the thrilling song of triumph with which "Miriam the Prophetess" and her maidens celebrated Israel's deliverance, it is said: "So Moses brought Israel from the Red Sea; and they went out into the wilderness of Shur." (Ex. xv. 22.) The word Shur in Hebrew signifies "a wall;" and as we stand at 'Ayún Músa and glance over the desert at the Jebels er Ráhah and et Tíh which border the gleaming plain, we at once appreciate the fact that these long wall-like escarpments are the chief if not the only prominent characteristics of this portion of the wilderness, and we need not wonder that the Israelites should have named this memorable spot, after its most salient feature, the wilderness of Shur or the wall. The Arabs, with their usual inconsistency, adopt two sites for the miracle—here, and at the Hammám Far'ún, or "Pharaoh's Hot Bath"—a frowning chalk cliff a little further down the coast. Pharaoh's unquiet spirit is still supposed to haunt the deep, and keep alive the boiling sulphurous spring which started up at his last angry drowning gasp. The sea at this point is called Birket Farún, or "Pharaoh's Lake." When asked how they can reconcile their accounts of Moses having crossed the sea at both these spots, the simple Bedawín answer, at least they did to me, "What seems remote to us is near to God Most High."

From the Wells of Moses we traversed an unvaried desert plain for three days; there is nothing to attract attention but the bleached camel-bones that mark the track, and nothing to afford food for reflection but the thought that, like the children of Israel, you too have gone "three days in the desert and have found no water." (Ex. xv. 22.) One object of rather melancholy interest you do pass at the outset of your march; it is a simple Arab grave, where some travellers a few years ago found the corpse of a Terbání Arab who "had been smitten with the yellow pest and fallen asleep by the roadside," and accorded it a hasty burial on the spot. It is now called Gabr es Seba'íy, "the Lad's Tomb," and gives its name to that portion of the Wády Merází in which it is situated.

On the third day we reached 'Ain Hawwárah, which most previous travellers have sought to identify with the Marah of Scripture. It is a solitary spring of bitter water with a stunted palm-tree growing near it, and affording a delicious shade. The quality of the water varies considerably at different times, and on the present occasion it was not only drinkable but palatable. It is, however, only fair to state that Mr Holland, who had visited the well on several former occasions, pronounced such purity of the water to be quite exceptional. The meaning "Fount of Destruction," given to the name *Hawárah* by Dr Robinson and all previous travellers, is, like the orthography, incorrect. The real name, Hawwárah, signifies a small pool, the water of which sinks into the soil by little and little, leaving the residue unfit to drink; a description eminently applicable to the spring in question. A few miles before reaching 'Ain Hawwárah we pass a large piece of detached rock lying by the roadside, and called Hajar er Rekkáb, or "the Rider's Mounting-stone." In a journey so featureless as this, every object, small or great, has its interest; and the Arabs will point the stone out to you with an air of conscious pride, as much as to say: "There, you poor benighted Frank, you can show nothing like that in *your* country." A little further on, the eye is again refreshed by the sight of green tamarisks and feathery palms, and just off the customary track is a pleasant stream of running water. This is Wády Gharandel, generally regarded as Elim, and whether or no the grove and stream are the lineal descendants of the twelve springs and seventy palm-trees which the Children of Israel found there, it is clear that the site of Elim must lie somewhere in the immediate neighbourhood. As it was Sunday, we halted here for the day, and, after morning service, proceeded to visit some "old houses" which the Arabs reported to exist in the neighbourhood. These proved to be ancient tombs excavated in the chalk cliffs, but had been so much disturbed, apparently by Arabs taking shelter in them, that, although some human bones and fragments of wood were discovered there, they were too much broken and displaced to render it possible to identify the position of the skeletons or determine the age to which they belonged. A jawbone and skull which presented some peculiarities of conformation were brought away. After this, we made our way down to the running stream before spoken of; and, insignificant though it was, it presented a refreshing sight to eyes that had been so long accustomed to the scorching white glare of the thirsty plains. At one point, a broken rock and a slight change in the level of the bed of the stream offered an opportunity for a bathe, which was eagerly taken advantage of and appreciated. The anticipated enjoyment of this luxury was enhanced by the contemplation of the beautiful, bright green grass which grew by the side of the brook, but alas! it was "like Dead Sea fruit, that tempts the eye," and turned to packing-needles and clothes-brushes on the sore and tender feet.

Early on the following morning we passed two

heaps of stones called Mangaz Hisân Abu Zena, "Abu Zena's Horse's Leap," concerning which the following legend was recounted to me by an old Bedawí of the 'Awârimeh tribe : "An Arab named Abu Zena was riding a mare that was with foal, and, notwithstanding her critical condition, was urging her along at a cruel speed. When she came to this spot he dug his spurs into her sides, whereupon the mare made a tremendous leap and fell down dead. Abu Zena, in wonder at the immense length of the stride which his horse had taken, marked the distance with two stones, and related the incident afterwards to his friends. The matter soon became noised abroad, and every Arab who passed that way with a comrade would discuss the marvellous leap and mark out the distance with a stone as Abu Zena himself had done, and thus the stone heaps grew. Admiration for the mare's performance soon increased with the pagan Arabs of that time, and she became at last an object of veneration, and was worshipped as a deity, offerings of corn being brought to the spot. But when they forsook idolatry for the worship of the true God, they came to look upon their former gods as devils, and turned their pagan observances into an expression of aversion for the demon whom they supposed to haunt the accursed spot. Thus, instead of the usual offering of corn, they would throw stones upon the heaps, and, kicking a little dust upon it with their feet, cry out, 'Eat *that*, and get thee gone!'" This custom is still kept up, and every one of our

Arabs as they passed the spot picked up a stone to cast upon the heap, and, kicking the dust over it contemptuously, cried: "*Agsa 'Allig*," "Begone, and feed!" The legend is interesting as showing that horses once existed in the peninsula; and it thus strengthens the probability that the country was at one time more fertile than it is now, for in its present state it would be quite impossible to rear or even keep them there. At this point we branched off into the upper route; some travellers, however, prefer to turn down Wády Taiyebeh, keeping along the sea-coast. This road, as well as the probable route taken by the Israelites, I shall discuss later on.

After this point, the character of the country begins to change, and we leave the dreary level plains of sand for more picturesque, though scarcely less desolate, mountain features. Traversing the broad, open valley of Useit, where there are also a few palm-trees and springs, and proceeding by a slightly devious route along Wády Hamr, we pitched our tents at the foot of the mountain called Sarbút el Jemel, which marks the commencement of the sandstone district. At a sharp bend in the valley, a little way past this spot, occur the first specimens of the famous Sinaitic Inscriptions. Another day's journey brought us to the mouth of Wády Nasb, the name of which, "the Valley of the Sacrificial Stone," suggests reminiscences of the old pagan rites of pre-Islamitic times. Here are great heaps of slag and other vestiges of the Egyptian miners who formerly colonised the place, and whose workings for copper, manganese, and turquoise cover the neighbouring sandstone hills. The corner of the valley is marked by a large rounded rock, which a little chiselling might turn into a formidable rival to the Egyptian sphinx, and which presents also a curious phenomenon to the geologist, for in the sandstone of the flat terraces surrounding it the ripple marks of primeval waves may still be seen. In the course of this day's march we met some Russian pilgrims returning from Sinai; four of them were women, one of whom had undertaken the long and tedious voyage in order to pay a tribute of respect to the memory of her husband, who had made his last pilgrimage there a year before. I subsequently saw the remains of the lamented deceased in a basket at the convent.

Leaving Wády Nasb we came in a few hours to the foot of Sarábít el Khádim, and alighted from our camels to visit the curious ancient Egyptian ruins on the summit of the mountain.

Much has already been written about this interesting spot, and as I too shall have something to say concerning it in a future chapter, I will content myself now with a mere passing notice. On the broad plateau of a sandstone mountain stands a little group of ruins containing a number of upright flat stones, with rounded tops, exactly similar in form to the conventional gravestones of a London cemetery. On closer inspection these, as well as the stones of which the walls were once composed, are found to be covered with hieroglyphics, and the ruins are in reality those of a temple (or rather temples, for there are two distinct buildings) erected for the convenience of the Egyptians who worked in the numerous mines around. The upper end contains the sanctuary, which is excavated out of the natural rock.

Our baggage camels had been sent on ahead while we turned aside to visit Sarábít el Khádim; and as it was necessary for us to reach the encampment before dark, we had not much time for moralising on the quaint aspect of this relic of an elaborate civilisation amongst the savage wilds of Sinai, nor for speculating upon the condition of that little knot of worshippers who mayhap were bowing down to Apis while the great Pilgrim Father passed, led onward by the cloud by day and fire by night. After a hurried glance, therefore, we descended the mountain and rode along through a narrow defile between sandstone cliffs called Nagb Súwig, encamping a little further on, in Wády Bark. The sun had already set before we came up to the tents, and I was thus enabled to enjoy the pleasure of a new sensation—that of a hungry man who sees a distant fire and knows it is his dinner which is being cooked. Alas! there is no romance that will stand the test of appetite.

The next day's march brought us to Wády Lebweh, which is approached by a steep and rugged pass, where we were shown the rude wall called Hait-el-Karnák (and sometimes el Membatch), which the Towarah Bedawín threw up to resist the Egyptian troops whom Mohammed 'Ali had sent to punish them for having intercepted and robbed a caravan of camels, laden with coffee and other merchandise, which was proceeding from Cairo to Suez. The outrage had been perpetrated as a sort of protest against what the Towarah considered an invasion of their rights and privileges, for they claimed to have the monopoly of the carriage of goods along this road, and the Egyptian merchants had begun to employ other tribes instead of them. A slight skirmish took place at this spot, in which the poor Bedawín were worsted, notwithstanding their fortification, and were compelled to seek shelter in the mountains, until the superior of the convent consented to proceed to Cairo in person and arrange for a reconciliation with the government. The Bedawín are, as a rule, honest and inoffensive enough, but they resent any attempt to enter their country without an escort from their own number, which simply means hiring the necessary camels from their tribe. On this occasion the Pasha of Egypt seems to have gained but slight satisfaction, for, as the Arabs told me, with great gusto, "the coffee went for nothing, the Arabs had eaten it." They had wisely consumed it all in their mountain-fastnesses while the articles of peace were being drawn up. This, and a subsequent escapade of a similar nature, have cost them dear; and a Bedawí sheikh, with tears in his eyes, bewailed to me the penury that was being brought upon his tribe by the exaction of a yearly tribute of nearly ten shillings, paid as compensation for the stolen goods; and I did not see him smile again until the sad recollection was effaced by the consoling thought that his neighbours, the Garrásheh, had to pay two pounds. How many of us has a like consolation supported in the worst of ills!

The Wády Lebweh is remarkable for nothing but a fine overhanging rock, with a narrow cleft, called Shagík el 'Ajúz, "the Old Woman's Cleft," in which is a deliciously cool spring; a little further on there is a quaint conical mountain, Zibb el Baheir Abu Baharíyeh, commanding, if not the finest, at least one of the most striking views in the peninsula. From this point the long white range of the Tíh mountains, the hills upon the African coast, and the mighty peaks of Serbál and Katarína are all distinctly visible; but that which lends most interest to the prospect is the striking view of the long granite wall of the Sinai mountain-group; this, although one of the most characteristic features in the conformation of the country, might escape the traveller's immediate notice from almost any other point of sight; here however it thrusts itself very forcibly upon him.

Later on in the same day we reached Wády Berráh, "the Valley of the Passer Out," a most appropriate name, as through two gigantic hills that stand at its lower end you pass out into the more open country which divides the sandstone district from the granite range.

In a small side wády to the left, as you enter this valley, is a lovely little spring, called Erthámeh; and on the right-hand side stands a gigantic mass of rock, which looks as if it might have been divided by a clean cut from another somewhat smaller boulder by its side. It is called Hajar el Laghweh, or, "the Speaking Stone." The legend runs, that Moses, coming with the Children of Israel along the valley, was stopped in his career by this rocky obstacle. His companion bade him smite it with his sword, but the prophet hesitated to essay so hopeless a task. A voice, however, was heard to proceed from the stone itself bidding him strike, which he accordingly did, and it was immediately cleft through from top to bottom, "as though it had been but a piece of flesh."

From Wády Berráh we emerge upon a large open space, the confluence of several important valleys, at the foot of the long granite wall which I have just mentioned as shutting off the central or Sinai group of mountains from the western portion of the peninsula. There are but three points at which this barrier is passable—Wády es Sheikh, the Nagb Hawa, and Wády Emleisah. Of these, the last is almost too rugged for foot-passengers, and the Nagb Hawa can only be traversed by lightly laden or riding camels. A large caravan like our own is therefore compelled to adopt the road by Wády es Sheikh, a broad open valley extending up to the base of Jebel Músa itself, and containing a fine grove of tamarisk trees, called Tarfat el Gidarain. The wády cuts right through the granitic wall, forming a narrow defile, with a tolerably level floor and lofty precipitous rocks on either side. In this gorge, which is called el Watíyeh, the Arabs shew a large detached rock, not unlike an arm-chair in shape, as the Magád en Nebí Músa, or Seat of the Prophet Moses. The legend does not relate the circumstances under which the Prophet occupied the seat in question, but a tall white-topped peak is also pointed out as the place where his sheep went up to graze. It is most probable that, like many other similar spots in the neighbourhood, the peculiar natural conformation has given rise to both the name and the story.

Mr Holland, who believes the route we are now following to have been that taken by the Israelites, suggests that this may be the site of Rephidim, and the rock in question the position occupied by Moses during the battle with the Amalekites. In many ways, it is true, the situation answers well to the description given in the Bible. We have just seen that el Watíyeh is the only practicable pass into the fertile district around Jebel Músa, and one which the Amalekites would consequently be desirous of holding against an invading force; there is also ample room for the encampment of either host, and, the pass once crossed, abundance of water within easy reach. The evidence, however, in favour of the identification of Feirán with Rephidim, and of the supposition that the Israelites took the lower route by the sea-coast is, as I shall presently shew, so strong that, while acknowledging the value of Mr Holland's suggestion, the other members of the expedition were unable to accept his hypothesis. From this point the journey lies entirely through granite rocks, the sharp rugged outlines of which, as well as the increasing height and sombre grey colouring of the mountains, impart much more of solemn grandeur to the scenery.

Near El Watíyeh is situated the tomb of Nebí Sáleh, a wretched little building, but accounted by the Bedawín one of the most sacred spots in the Peninsula. Hither they resort in great numbers at a certain season of the year to perform those ceremonies and sacrificial rites which I shall hereafter describe.

Who and what was Nebí Sáleh, "the Prophet Sáleh," or, as his name implies, "the Righteous Prophet"? A great saint with the Bedawín, perhaps the ancestor of the Sawálibeh tribe, who are named after him; but this explanation is vague and unsatisfactory, and in the absence of any certain information upon the subject I will venture to propound a theory. I must premise that near the summit of Jebel Músa is a peculiar mark in the stone which bears a strong resemblance to the imprint of a camel's foot. It is regarded by the Bedawín with great veneration, and the girls, when tending their flocks on the mountains, often milk their goats into it as a sure means of obtaining increase and prosperity. This mark is called Athar Nágat en Nebí, "the Footprint of the Prophet's She-camel." It is generally taken for granted that the Prophet in question is Mohammed, but to my mind there are several circumstances which seem to connect the Nebí Sáleh of the tomb with the Prophet of the legend. A

Bedawí's notions of the separate identity of Moses, Elias, and Sáleh are of the vaguest kind, and if asked to which of his national saints the camel belonged, you will find that he has never even thought of the question at all. There is no point in attributing the mysterious footprint to the camel of Mohammed, for the celebrated "night journey" to heaven, the prophet's only recorded aeronautic trip, was performed on Borák, a creature with the feet of a mule. But Mohammed has a legend in the Corán of a certain "Nebí Sáleh," who was sent as a prophet to the people of Thamúd, and whose divine mission was attested by the miraculous production of *a she-camel* from the rock.* The author of "El Islám" certainly did visit the Sinaitic mountains, and may in all probability have taken the story from the national traditions of the Peninsula. The origin and history of Nebí Sáleh is quite unknown to the present Bedawín inhabitants, but they nevertheless regard him with more *national* veneration than even Moses himself. I should therefore conclude that the Nebí Sáleh of the tomb in Wády es Sheikh, the Prophet of the camel's footprint and the Sáleh of the Corán are identical, and that the "people of Thamúd" are the Saracen inhabitants of Sinai, who preceded the Mohammedan invasion. Who then *was* Nebí Sáleh? Looking at the veneration in which his memory is held, and at the character of the miracle attributed to him—the rock smitten with a rod, and a live

* See Appendix B.

camel, the greatest of Bedawí blessings, miraculously produced therefrom—with the subsequent rebellion of the people for whom the Prophet worked the sign, I fancy that we may recognise in the tradition a distorted reminiscence of the history of the Israelitish lawgiver himself.

From the tomb of Nebí Sáleh we caught our first glimpse of the mountains of the Jebel Músa range. Our entrance into the Desert of Sinai was marked by a singularly appropriate incident, and we had a piece of the Bible translated for us into every-day life as it was in the time of the Patriarchs. We had reached the neighbourhood of the tents of our Sheikh 'Eid, and his wife and two children, accompanied by an aged male relative, came out to meet him. 'Eid saluted the old man, embraced him, and kissed him on either cheek, and the pair then, with right hands clasped, repeated over and over again the words *Taiyibin?* "Are you well?" with the answer *Al hamdu lilláh taiyibin*, "Thank God, well!" As I watched the scene, I could not help calling to mind the words of Exodus (xviii. 5—7): "And Jethro, Moses' father in law, came with his sons and his wife unto Moses in the wilderness, where he had encamped before the mount of God: And he said unto Moses, I thy father in law Jethro am come unto thee with thy wife and her two sons with her. And Moses went out to meet his father in law, and did obeisance, and kissed him, and they asked each other of their welfare; and they came into the tent."

FROM SUEZ TO SINAI.

Two more turns in the valley brought us to the mouth of Wády ed Deir—to the foot of Sinai.

Let us halt for a moment to contemplate the impressive scene, and meditate upon the sacred associations that gather round it. Before us lies a narrow valley, between two huge blocks of granite mountains and closed in at the upper end by a conical green hill. The two peaks which form the posterns of this valley are, respectively, on the left, Jebel ed Deir, "the Convent Mount": and, on the right, Rás Sufsáfeh, "the Willow Peak."

THE RÁS SUFSÁFEH FROM THE PLAIN.

The last is Mount Sinai itself—the very mountain, in all human probability, upon which "the Glory of the Lord rested in the sight of all the people." A stately, awful-looking, isolated mass it is, rearing its giant brow above the plain, as if in scornful contemplation of the world beneath. What scene so fitting to witness the proclamation of the primeval law as those hoary primeval rocks? Surely it was not accident which determined the choice, but rather that universal harmony of the Moral and the Physical in Nature which attest so plainly the unity of purpose in God's creative scheme.

At the base of the bluff is a long semicircular mound, forming a sort of amphitheatre, from which a select congregation of elders might obtain a nearer view of the mountain. The full proportions of the Rás Sufsáfeh are best seen from the approach by the great plain of Er Ráhah.

Proceeding up the valley, you pass, on your left, the hill on which Aaron is supposed to have set up the golden calf, and which is still called after him; next by some old monastic ruins, and the now deserted barracks of 'Abbás Pasha's soldiery, and, then following the path which they constructed, in a few minutes reach the convent walls. As you approach, your Arabs set up a shout of *Yá Músa* (for the porter's name is Moses), a little wicket in the wall opens, and a turbaned head appears and asks your business at the convent. A rope is let down, to which you attach your letter of introduction from the branch convent at Cairo, and, as it is drawn up, other faces—white, handsome, and vacant—appear and salute you, either with pantomimic gestures, or in a language of their own composing, fondly imagined by the community to represent Arabic.

Presently there issues forth from the gate at the side an old gentleman, reverend though fuddled in mien, dignified though unsteady in gait,—with a patriarchal beard, and the most mediæval of serge costumes, who, if such attention be not dexterously avoided, will fall upon your neck and greet you with a paternal kiss.

This is Brother Jacobus, the œconomos, or bursar, of the convent, once a flourishing Smyrna merchant, but now, either because he is tired of the world, or, more probably, because the world is tired of him, brought here to end his days in the Convent of Mount Sinai. "I was an unbeliever," said he to me one day, "until I came and saw what a holy place this is. For, when the earthquake shakes the mountains round, it never moves a thing within the convent walls; and that convinced me." As an earthquake has not taken place here within the memory of man, this test of the sanctity of the establishment can hardly be called a crucial one.

It was by this worthy that the members of the Sinai Expedition were ushered into the Convent of St Katharine.

CHAPTER IV.

THE CONVENT OF MOUNT SINAI.

Foundation and name. Exterior of the Convent. We are introduced to the "brethren." Character of the monks. The Interior. Strangers' apartments. The Mosque. The Church : Chapel of the Burning Bush. The Mount of the Cross. Russian pilgrims. The Library and Archbishop's room. The Refectory. The gardens and Cemetery. Arab servants. Arab traditions relating to the Convent.

THE Convent of Mount Sinai, according to popular tradition, owes its origin to the Byzantine Emperor Justinian, who fortified and endowed the little church built by Helena, the mother of Constantine, "on the spot where God spake with Moses." It was at first dedicated to the Transfiguration, until the removal thither of the relics of St Katharine gave that lady a share in the patronage ; and it has since then been generally called the Convent of St Katharine.

Amidst the cold grey hues and deep shadows of the mountains, rise up the graceful forms of tapering cypress trees, and their dark rich foliage is thrown into harmonious contrast with the lighter verdure of the poplars which grow beside them, and with the varied tints of the olive and almond trees that peep above the wall. Sheltered behind this lovely garden is the monastery, looking very calm and peaceful, and suggesting nothing of the nest of dirt and ignorance within.

It is an ancient castellated building, the eastern side, which faces the valley, presenting a flat wall composed of large blocks of hewn granite, partly original masonry and partly restored. About thirty feet from the ground is a small wicket covered with a penthouse, like those seen in English mills; through this travellers were formerly drawn up into the Convent, though they are now admitted by a side door. A little farther to the south is a buttress tower built by General Kleber, the commander of the French troops during their occupation of Egypt. A white tablet let into the wall commemorates the restoration of the building by that officer. In the angles which this buttress forms with the wall are some small niches chiselled out in the stones, and these contain rude pans of incense, placed there by the Arabs, who venerate the Prophet Khidhr (or Elias) at this spot. On the north side is a large door, now blocked up, called Báb er Ráïs, or the Abbot's gate. By it the bishops used to enter, and from it a distribution of clothes and food to every member of the Jibalíyeh tribe was made on his arrival. It is now finally closed, but the practice of distributing alms, on the appointment of a new superior or the arrival of an archbishop, is still kept up.

GATE OF THE CONVENT OF ST KATHARINE.

Strongly fortified though the convent is by its stout massive walls, it is ill adapted for withstanding a determined attack, being easily commanded from either side of the valley. Indeed we learn from the old records of the place that the Bedawin, who have from time to time manifested a laudable antipathy to monastic institutions, were in the habit of occasionally stoning or shooting the reverend fathers from the heights above.

A large iron gate leads into the courtyard, at the upper end of which is an unfinished modern building, commenced by some Russian masons, and intended for the accommodation of travellers and pilgrims. On the left or north side of the convent, is the original entrance; the door has been blocked up, and consists of a flat arch or lintel surmounted by a macciacoulis, on which is a Roman tablet containing a now illegible inscription, apparently the oldest in the building.

The entrance into the building is by a small wicket gate of massive iron studded with antiquated nails, behind which is a subterranean way into the garden. Passing this little door, through a low intricate passage and by the church and mosque, we come into what may be called the lobby of the place, at the northern end of which, up a rickety wooden staircase, is situated the œconomos' room.

Hither we followed our guide, to be entertained by him with coffee and date brandy ('*araki*) and introduced to such of the monks and priests as had dropped in to see the newly-arrived guests. These were the *élite* of the community, and during our subsequent stay at Jebel Músa we saw a great deal of them; I will therefore describe them more particularly. As became the aristocracy, they were better dressed than their brethren; but magnanimous would be the Israelite who might purchase their wardrobe, unless indeed he had received an unlimited order for the supply of scarecrows, or had a permanent contract as *costumier* to a travelling wax-work van. First there was Father Galaktion, the librarian, and therefore my particular friend. Then came Father Gabriel, in church a solemn, handsome minister, with a sonorous voice and the demeanour of a saint; elsewhere a good-tempered, giggling imbecile, with a taste for mislearning European names. Gabriel often winks, a wise, humorous wink to outward appearance, but really proceeding from nothing but exuberant sociability, for his mental capacity is beyond a joke, or rather not equal to one. A sour-looking Wallachian priest, the interpreter for Russian pilgrims; Janidios, a hook-nosed priest; a doting old man with a beard like a pantaloon, whose sole occupation consists in mumbling the lessons in church and humming songs to the tame ibex in the courtyard of the mosque—these made up the party who were present at our reception. There were a few others of the monks, whose idiosyncrasies merit a passing word. Amongst them were Brother Kallostratos, the porter, whose appearance in England on the 5th of November would most assuredly subject him to immolation on a funeral pyre; and Kyrillos, a fat, cunning monk, uniting in his own person the attributes of gardener and baker, whose chief object of devotion was the rum bottle, and whose religious exercise consisted in lonely pilgrimages to the mountain, in pursuit of partridges which he might not eat. Nor must I omit to mention the carpenter, but *his* true effigy you may see any day by inquiring at a toy-shop for a German nutcracker. Another interesting inmate is a mad tailor from Constantinople, who, having been driven out of his senses by the just indignation of a pasha whom he was hardy enough to press for payment of his little bill, adopted the only walk of life left open to him, and turned monk.

I had hoped that in such a place as Sinai there

might still linger some trace of that devotion which seems to have characterized the recluses of old; some religious enthusiasm which should atone for their having fled from the duties of that state of life to which it has pleased God to call them. But no! I found in them no enthusiasm, no hopes, no aspirations—no care for anything but indolence and rum. They even neglect the only duty which they have left themselves to perform, and the services in the fine old church are almost unattended, except when some Russian pilgrims come and call forth the mock piety and grumblings of the monks.

They do keep up, these holy fathers, a semblance of that charity which made the abbeys of old so famous, and every morning they dispense with an ungrudging hand loaves of bread to any Arab that chooses to apply. One of these loaves I brought back with me; an eminent geologist to whom I submitted it pronounced it "a piece of metamorphic rock containing fragments of quartz embedded in an amorphous paste." No decently brought up ostrich could swallow one without endangering his digestion for the term of his natural life.

The ceremony of introduction over, we proceeded to read, or rather translate, a letter which we had brought with us from Sir Henry James, setting forth the objects of the Sinai Expedition, and requesting the acceptance by the fraternity of copies of the books, photographs, and models relating to the survey of Jerusalem; after which weighty piece of business we took a preliminary glance round the monastery.

Passing out of the œconomos' room, you ascend by a rude staircase, leading past the flat roof or terrace on which the monks take the air, to a long gallery of rooms designed for the accommodation of travellers and pilgrims. The wall which faces you at the top of the first flight is pierced with loopholes, through which fine little glimpses may be caught of the mountains and the magnificent plain of Er Ráhah beyond. In these are set the ordnance of the convent—pieces varying in size from that of the common pistol to a foot or so in length, and mounted upon the roughest carriages. Small as they are, it would require no inconsiderable amount of pluck to fire off these formidable pieces of artillery, for it would puzzle even an Armstrong to predict at which end the discharge might take place.

Half the rooms in this gallery are reserved for travellers, and are tolerably clean apartments, furnished with a table in the centre and cushions placed on the divans all round; some of them have even the luxury of an iron bedstead. The pilgrims are lodged in a much less ceremonious way, and are left to make themselves as comfortable as they can, packed six or eight together, in little rooms, with mattresses placed upon the floor.

From the door of his room the traveller can see all over the interior of the convent, which consists of a series of irregular buildings on different levels; and in the midst of them, side by side, rise up the church and the mosque—a strange conjunction in such a place.

The mosque has a peculiarly shabby and whitewashed appearance, which contrasts strikingly with the neat and respectable façade of the church, though the effect of the latter is spoilt by its being built below the level of the other buildings, so that from the balcony only the gable end of it is seen. To the right are the buildings occupied by the monks, much resembling a row of almshouses.

The only present guardian of the mosque is a tame *bedan* or ibex, who resides with his wife and family in the courtyard. A fine, well-fed, bearded fellow he is, with long curved horns, and a high-spirited beast withal, as Captain Palmer and I found to our cost when we invaded his domain. We had entered the mosque and closed the door after us, when the ibex, whose food is kept in the building, was seized with evident misgivings as to the integrity of our motives, and suspecting us of designs upon his beans dived violently into the place, and proceeded to execute a series of startling evolutions expressive of indignation and contempt. After a graceful *pas-seul*, he butted wildly at us, and was with difficulty dragged and pushed outside; even then he was far from giving in; but as I hastened to undo the gate, Captain Palmer performed an involuntary waltz round the yard, and, enticing him cunningly towards the gate, slipped out, and had just time to shut it after him, when the animal, with the shrill peculiar whistle which it always utters when disturbed, made one last futile charge and well-nigh brought the palings to the ground.

The story of the building of the mosque is that, at the time of the great destruction of monasteries by the Saracens throughout the East, the monks at Sinai received intelligence of the approach of the commander who was to execute the order, and ran up this building, which proved the salvation of the place.

They declare, also, that they possessed at one time a charter, given them by Mohammed himself and signed with the impression of his own hand, promising them perpetual immunity and protection. This document the Sultan Selim is said to have taken with him to Constantinople, and to have deposited in the library there, granting the monks in return a fresh firman confirming all their rights and privileges.

The church is a fine old building, generally ascribed to Justinian, but certainly not earlier than the time of Theodosius, and the interior is a very imposing specimen of Greek ecclesiastical decoration. The Greek Church abjures devotional images, but amply makes up for the loss by covering every available inch of space with gaudy paintings and tinsel ornaments. Of these the convent church contains some very elaborate and curious specimens. Over the apse is a beautiful piece of mosaic, representing the scene of the Transfiguration: at the corners of this are two medallions, which have been generally supposed to be portraits of Justinian and Theodora, but which are

THE CONVENT OF MOUNT SINAI.

more probably, judging from their peculiar characteristics, intended for our Lord and the Virgin Mary. From the ceiling hang numerous silver lamps suspended by long cords, and these, with the elaborate workmanship of every article of church furniture in the place, produce a very beautiful and striking effect.

The great attraction, however, is the Chapel of the Burning Bush, a little oratory at the east end of the building. An altar, overlaid with a beautifully chased silver plate, stands upon the spot where the sacred bush is supposed to have grown, and the lamps upon this are never allowed to be extinguished. Over the altar is a little window, shedding a dim, mysterious light, that well befits so solemn a spot. It is said that the sunlight only penetrates it one day in the year, and then a solitary ray darts through a cleft in the mountain above and falls upon the chapel-floor. The cleft is marked by a wooden cross, and the mountain is accordingly called by the Arabs Jebel es Salíb (the Mount of the Cross). This fact, or fancy, has given rise to a curious Arab legend. They say that once upon a time the Book of Moses, which had been delivered to him by God on the top of Sinai, was kept upon the summit of the mountain, and then the rain fell round about for alternate periods of forty days and forty nights. But the monks, wishing to obtain greater control over the Arabs, brought down the mysterious book, which was engraved upon stone, and built it into the walls of the church, leaving this little window through which it might be occasionally seen. Whenever they desire rain, they have only to open the window to procure it at once, and they can even bring wind and storms and locusts upon the country by the same means.

In all the representations of the Burning Bush the Virgin Mary and Child are depicted as occupying the centre of the flame, the Greek theory being that the mystery typified in that revelation was the virginity of the mother of our Lord.

Before entering the Chapel of the Burning Bush, the visitor is requested in so many words "to take the shoes from off his feet, as the place whereon he is standing is holy ground." The late 'Abbás Pasha was so much impressed with the sanctity of the shrine that during his sojourn at Sinai he preferred saying his daily prayers upon its soft carpeted floor to prostrating himself upon the hard pavement of the whitewashed mosque. There are other chapels in the Convent designed for the use of the Latin and Armenian sects, but as only Greek and Mohammedan pilgrims now visit the place they have become entirely deserted.

A Greek service is not by any means imposing; it is hurried through in so slovenly a manner as to suggest painful doubts whether it might not be performed equally well, Thibetan fashion, by machinery. I was present on several occasions when Russian pilgrims attended the convent church. After the levity and indolence of the monks, it was quite refreshing to witness the devotion of these poor, unkempt, anxious serfs. They gaze with rapturous

THE CONVENT OF MOUNT SINAI.

veneration upon all around them, kiss the pictures and the priests, and rap their heads upon the marble floor with wild and resonant enthusiasm. With many of them this pilgrimage is the realisation of a long life's dream, and to accomplish it they undergo unheard-of toils and privations. Aided by small contributions from a public fund, they set off, frequently from the remotest parts of Russia, and proceed on foot to Odessa, stopping for rest and food at the various convents which line the road. Thence long weary journeys by ship, rail and camels bring them to Sinai; and, after being trotted up and down the mountain, and taken round to all the sacred spots, they are sent back to Alexandria, to be again shipped to Jaffa, *en route* for Jerusalem. Arrived at the holy city, they proceed to wash off their sins by dipping, clothes and all, into the Jordan; and this is in most instances their first wash since leaving the land of the Czar.

The pilgrims stay at the convent eight days. When they are on the point of departure, every Arab who presents himself with his camel can claim a certain portion of the hire, whether he be employed or not. This custom has been long established, and is kept up to the present day. The monks, moreover, are bound to give notice to their *ghufara*, or "protectors," of the presence of pilgrims at the convent, and this is done in the following manner. A man is despatched to the well in Wády Nasb, on the upper route, who plants two footmarks in the direction of the convent, and places in front of them the Jibalíyeh tribe-mark. Any Arab who happens to pass that way and see the sign may present himself at the convent and share in the profits of the transport.

But to return to the description of the interior. Leaving the church, we came to the library, a wretched unpainted room, containing a goodly number of worm-eaten manuscript volumes in Greek and Arabic. They are chiefly patristic or controversial literature, and of little interest, the really valuable books being securely locked up in the Archbishop's room, into which we were not at the time allowed to penetrate. I offered to make a catalogue of the Arabic manuscripts, and had actually commenced the task, but so many difficulties were thrown in my way that I was at length compelled to relinquish it. Father Jacob, the œconomos, looked upon the whole proceeding as fatuous from the very first. Since the affair of the Codex Sinaiticus, the monks have come to regard their manuscript treasures with a jealous eye, though not from any real appreciation of their literary value. They ought, however, to be content, for the Emperor Alexander has paid them handsomely for it, and presented them in addition with a bran new shrine for good St Katharine's bones. Considering the worm-eaten and utterly neglected state of the books, I think that it would be greatly to the gain of literature if the whole collection were handed over to more careful guardianship.

One day, as I was turning over some old volumes of patristric lore, the librarian came up to me with glee and announced that he had discovered a book which must prove of the greatest interest to me. It was, "Jane Shore, a tragedie for Drury Lane Theatre."

On the occasion of a subsequent visit to Sinai, I succeeded in gaining admittance to the Archbishop's apartments, a fine suite of rooms consisting, among others, of an old fashioned reception chamber and a private chapel gorgeously decorated with arabesque work. Here the most valuable part of the MS. treasures are kept, some of which I examined. The well-known Codex Aureus is a beautifully-written copy of the four Gospels, containing illuminated portraits of the Evangelists and other sacred personages. It is attributed to the Emperor Theodosius, the colophon giving the date and transcriber's name in the abbreviated Uncial characters. A collation of this MS. would no doubt be a valuable addition to New Testament criticism, although the date, about the eight century, which is assigned to it, is not sufficiently remote to give it any very high authority. A person exercising tact, and remaining sufficiently long at the convent, might copy, and perhaps photograph, every leaf. I endeavoured to impress upon the monks that no other design prompts an investigation of their books than that of benefiting sacred literature by a description of the works in their possession. There are other very interesting volumes in the collection; among them an ancient copy of the Psalms in Georgian, written on papyrus, and another curious copy of the Psalms, written in a small female hand on six small pages, but without a date. Amongst a pile of patristic and other works, of no great age or interest, are some curious old Syriac books and one or two palimpsests. My hurried visit prevented me from examining these with any great care; but they would no doubt well repay investigation. The proximity of the convent to civilized parts, the frequent intercourse of the monks with European scholars and travellers, and more especially the renown of the Codex Sinaiticus, are causes that militate strongly against any chance of procuring much more of bibliographical interest from Sinai, although a thorough examination of the library would doubtless yield some valuable results.

We next visited the refectory, a narrow room approached by a long dusty corridor on the southern side of the building. It contains two ancient tables, of rude but elaborate construction, which extend along its entire length, as well as a small pulpit and a gaudy altar at the upper end. The scene when the monks are at dinner is indescribably quaint, and seems to carry us back centuries, to the times of the Crusaders, whose arms and crests are scratched with their dagger points upon the doors. There they are, some twenty long-bearded men with serge dresses and rosaries, just as you may see them in the paintings of the old Italian masters, eating their vegetable diet in silence on the uncovered board, while a priest from the pulpit is drawling out in a monotonous tone the life of some saint appropriate to the day. Behind them stand the servitors, only to be distinguished from the rest by being, if possible, a little dirtier and a little more villainous than their brethren; and at the lower table some half-dozen or so of pilgrims are munching lettuces with faces expressive of mingled hunger and awe. When the monks have finished their repast the cats of the convent (and their name is legion) assemble at the ringing of a bell and receive their rations from the scraps that are left. Near the door is the kitchen, and a little farther on the distillery, where that most important adjunct to a recluse's life, the 'araki, is made. A carpenter's shop, a bakehouse and other offices, numerous small chapels situated in odd corners of the convent, and one or two pretty little oriental wells, complete the category.

The whole effect of the interior of the convent is peaceful and picturesque, and the background is simply magnificent. On the left is Jebel ed Deir, with its rugged, pathless sides, and upon a ledge, where the green markings on the smooth surface of the rocks indicate the presence of water, there springs up from a heap of stones (the ruined convent of St Episteme) a solitary cypress; anywhere else this would look an imposing tree, but here it seems a mere dark-green thread against the glowing grey of the mountain-side. On the right rises the shoulder of the Jebel Músa block, stern and gigantic as its neighbour, and in the opening between these wondrous walls the green round summit of Jebel Moneijáh stands out in bold relief against the sky.

Of the garden I have already spoken: it is laid out rather for use than ornament, and has little beauty beside the foliage of its trees. There are many other such in the neighbourhood of the convent which once formed part of smaller monastic establishments that have long since disappeared. To these the monks of Sinai claim an exclusive right, allowing a certain percentage of the produce to the Arab families who tend them. As they take no measures to ensure their cultivation, and only demand that their Arab tenant should bring them a few vegetables or fruit from time to time, this arrangement tends rather to prevent than to promote horticulture—an occupation which, if only properly encouraged, might be made an important instrument in ameliorating the condition of the Bedawín, especially in the well-watered valleys around Jebel Músa. But what do the Greek monks care whether the Bedawín starve or no? A Christian community—Heaven save the mark!—they have resided here for centuries without learning one jot of the language or life of their neighbours, without teaching them one word of religion or truth.

In the midst of the gardens is situated the crypt, where the monks are buried, or rather stacked away, after their decease. It is a curious and ghastly sight. The defunct bishops are brought here and stowed away in what I at first took for cigar-boxes; and a few hermits of unusual sanctity are hung up in bags, like hams, against the wall. There are two compartments in this mansion of the dead—one for the priests, the other for the lay brethren; and seated against the low iron door which connects the two, is a dried and crouching figure, the mortal remains of a certain St Stephanos, who was porter at the convent some three hundred years ago. He sits there still, in hideous mockery of his former office; and, as if to make his appearance still more ghastly, some Russian pilgrims have decked him out in a silk shirt and gaudy skull-cap. In one of the boxes are the remains of two hermits, sons of an Indian king, the legend says, who lived and died upon the mountains, in adjoining cells. Their skeletons are still connected by the chain which bound them together in life, and which was so contrived, that when one lay down to rest his neighbour was dragged up to pray, so that one of them was ever watchful at his post.

It was quite a relief to me to come out of this gloomy vault into the bright sunlight and pure mountain air once more; and as I thought upon the sad memorials of the frailty of human life, and the still sadder evidences of benighted superstition marring the fair likeness of God in man, a new and real sense seemed to be given to the words which first met my eye as I issued forth from the vault, a Greek legend inscribed on an empty coffin:

ΜΑΤΑΙΟΤΗΣ ΜΑΤΑΙΟΤΗΤΩΝ ΠΑΝΤΑ ΜΑΤΑΙΟΤΗΣ.

Vanity of Vanities, all is Vanity.

The Arab servants of the convent are fine sturdy fellows, and present a great contrast to their effeminate masters. Mohammed, the chief amongst them, is a good-looking, stalwart Arab, always ready to lend the traveller or his servants a hand; nor is Músa, the next most prominent of the attendants, less willing or obliging, and, notwithstanding the loss of a finger, blown off by a matchlock, he is handy too. There is quite a colony of them in the convent-garden, where their tents are pitched; and the pilgrim who wishes to add to his entomological stores, cannot do better than give a few piastres and a pickle bottle for the collection of Coleoptera to little Mohammed and Khidhr, the respective heirs of the two last-named Arabs.

They all belong to the Jibalíyeh tribe, who are recognised as the serfs of the convent. This tribe is said to be of European origin, and to have descended from the colony of Wallachian and Egyptian slaves, placed there by Justinian to protect the monks. They themselves have a tradition that they came from a country called "K'láh;" and their features, differing somewhat from the ordinary Bedawí type, would seem to favour the supposition. The Jibalíyeh have an additional claim upon our interest as the representatives of the older inhabitants of Sinai. The remaining Bedawín tribes have preserved the purity of descent, and the genealogical pride, which is so curious a characteristic of the Desert races; and in names, manners, and appearance, they are now what their ancestors were in

Hejjáz or Yemen. It is clear that they can have
no admixture of Aramæan blood; and if any of the
ancient local traditions do still survive in the peninsula,
it is to the Jibalíyeh alone that we owe their
perpetuation.

The convent, forming, as it were, the nucleus
around which almost all the traffic of the peninsula
clusters, has become an object of the greatest interest
to the Bedawín, especially to those tribes to
whom the right of conducting pilgrims belongs.

The Arabs' notions of history and chronology
being necessarily of the vaguest kind, they regard
this convent as a relic of the remotest antiquity,
and not unnaturally associate it with their traditions
of Moses, the great patron saint of Sinai. Their
account of the building of the convent is, that when
Moses and the children of Israel arrived at the entrance
to the Nagb Hawa, the narrow pass leading
on to the great plain of Er Ráhah which stretches
in front of Mount Sinai, he determined to build a
monastery, in commemoration of their signal deliverance
from the hands of Pharaoh. But on the
following morning his chief workman found that
all the masons' tools had disappeared, and subsequent
research discovered that they had been miraculously
conveyed away, and deposited in Wády
Sho'eib, or "Jethro's Valley." Here then Moses,
in obedience to the omen which he had received,
laid the foundation of the present convent, and it
was subsequently completed by his daughter, St
Katharine. The origin of this incongruous legend

is probably due to the existence of some curious stone circles at the mouth of the pass, which apparently denote primeval burials, and are now called Matabb ed Deir el Gadím, "the site of the ancient monastery."

As well as the tradition of the Book of Moses, which I have before mentioned, the Arabs have many curious superstitions connected with the establishment. They suppose that it is under the special protection of heaven, and that no evil designs against it can ever prosper, but will recoil upon the aggressor's head. This is a very convenient doctrine, and was no doubt propagated by the monks, to restrain the lawless instincts of their neighbours the Bedawín, who, if report speaks truly, were formerly troubled with no such scruples. The treasures of the convent they believe to be of fabulous amount; these are kept securely locked in the cellars of the convent, the doors of which can only be opened by the simultaneous application of separate keys, in the possession of different members of the community. One of these subterranean chambers is guarded by so mysterious a power, that any one entering it would be at once struck down dead; and as it is not generally known which is the fatal door, no Arab would be found hardy enough to make the attempt upon any room in the building. The convent is in reality exceedingly wealthy, possessing large estates in Greece. The extent of its property in Sinai itself is said to include all lands lying within a radius of three days' journey from Jebel

Músa. The monks are supposed to owe their security to the potency of a charm which they possess, to wit, the cross; and so convinced are the Bedawín of the efficacy of this, that they themselves make frequent use of the same emblem, wearing it in their turbans, carrying it in their religious processions, and even occasionally placing it at the head of a tomb.

My own intimate association with the Bedawín of Sinai in the course of two protracted visits to the peninsula, has afforded me exceptionally favourable opportunities for studying the habits of this singular people. As the information which I thus gained is not only interesting in itself, but indispensable to the proper understanding of much that follows, I will devote a chapter to the life and character of the Towarah Arabs.

CHAPTER V.

THE BEDAWÍN OF SINAI.

Arab life and character. Social relations. Means of livelihood, dress, habits, health, &c. Numbers and origin. Officers and constitution; marriage; love; children; circumcision; burial; religion; sacrifices; festivals; saints; superstitions.

WHILE every other part of the world has witnessed innumerable changes, the desert alone seems to have escaped all innovation; and I believe that, not only in manners and mode of life, but even in dress and speech, the sons of Ishmael are now what they were in the days of the Patriarchs. The idea prevalent in Europe of the nomade character of the Arabs is erroneous. They are generally described as wandering incessantly with their tents from place to place, but in reality no people wander less than the Bedawín, or are more attached to their native homes. Arabic indeed is almost the only language besides our own in which the word "home," *watan*, can be expressed.

They have their winter and summer camping grounds, and, except to remove from one to the other as the season requires, they seldom change their residence. When travelling, they never make use of their tents, but sleep in the open air, merely wrapping their cloaks around them. Their encampments are not unlike those of the gipsies of this country, but the inhabitants are more wild and picturesque. The women, wrapped in their dark-blue mantles, grinding corn in primitive handmills, or weaving the materials of which the tents are composed, the children, dogs and goats playing about with a happy community of ideas, the men lazily drinking coffee and smoking, form a scene at once picturesque and amusing.

GROUP OF SINAI BEDAWIN.

Another misconception is that all Arabs are habitual robbers and murderers. It is true that, in the case of a strange or hostile tribe, or of an unauthorised intruder upon their own particular territory, their ideas of the rights of property do not accord with our own; but amongst themselves, or towards those who have entrusted themselves to their guardianship, their honesty and faith is unimpeachable; while, thanks to the terrible rigour of the "Vendetta" or blood-feud, homicide is far rarer in the desert than in civilised lands.

Although romance and war are intimately associated with our ideas of Arab character, we shall look in vain amongst the inhabitants of the desert for any such annals as the chivalry of Europe has produced. They have no history, because they have no nationality. Their country, their mode of life, produce a kind of clanship among the members of individual tribes, and perhaps of sympathy with the rest of the race, but here these ties end. They have not even a social, much less a political, organization. Circumstances may, and sometimes do, arise when concerted action, or the intervention of an acknowledged arbitrator, are necessary; and custom has provided for such emergencies by the establishment of the Sheikh and the 'Agyd, the civil and military chiefs. But, the necessity over and the crisis past, an Arab of the desert submits himself to no one, and owns no earthly lord or master but his own sovereign will. In the desert of Sinai and other places where European influence has penetrated, this statement must be slightly modified, for a Túrí's or a Maghrabí's religious and political creed may be

summed up in the precept, "Fear God and the
Consul." The Bedawín in their social relations present a favourable contrast to the more civilised inhabitants of the towns and villages of the East.
Their simple food, and the pure uncontaminated air
which they breathe, induce a healthful condition
both of body and mind. They are cheerful and even
inclined to jocularity, often enduring the greatest
hardships and privations without a murmur at their
lot. Their demeanour is courteous and gentle in
a marked degree, and the little punctilios of
etiquette and hospitality observed when Bedawín
meet would not fall far short of a Chesterfield's
standard. It must nevertheless be confessed that
when they do dispute, which almost invariably happens when money is the point at issue, they are as
violent, demonstrative and abusive as the most advanced civilisation could desire. In striking a bargain, an Arab will not hesitate to lie and overreach
you by every means in his power; but, when the
terms are once agreed upon, you may be perfectly
assured that his word is his bond. Theft and fraud
are absolutely unknown in Sinai.

Of the character and position of the women I
shall speak more fully when illustrating the rites and
ceremonies of marriage amongst the Towarah. They
are generally employed in the more menial and
domestic duties, grinding the corn, weaving the
goat's hair into the material of which the tents are
composed, preparing their husbands' meals, setting
the tent in order, and the like. The unmarried girls

tend the flocks and take them to pasture, such an occupation being considered derogatory to the dignity of a male. As with most Eastern nations, an extraordinary amount of respect is paid by the younger children to their parents, a boy not even daring to sit down or eat in his father's presence. As soon, however, as he is old enough and strong enough to battle with life for himself, the Bedawí youth throws off this allegiance, and treats his father afterwards with but little deference, looking upon himself in every way as an equal. The men are of course the bread-winners of the tribe, but their means of livelihood are scanty and inadequate. Their camels are their chief support, and a more destitute condition can scarcely be imagined than that of a Bedawí who does not possess one. The conveyance of travellers, pilgrims, stores, &c. to the Convent is an important item in the traffic of the Peninsula, but is uncertain, and confined to the few tribes who are the legitimate *ghufará* or "protectors." A small trade is also carried on with Suez and Cairo, the Arabs taking in charcoal, millstones, ibex-horns, gum-arabic, &c., and selling them to buy corn and tobacco. Some few, who live in the more fertile districts, such as Feirán, possess little pieces of ground, in which they grow tobacco and sell or barter it to their neighbours. The date-bearing palms in Feirán and elsewhere are each the property of individuals, and their fruit forms an important article of food with the Towarah. Those who possess flocks of sheep and goats make use of the hair and wool, and in spring time of their milk; they seldom slaughter them except for sacrifice.

Another article of commerce with them is *munn* or manna, which is a gummy saccharine substance, exuding from the *tarfah* or tamarisk tree. It continues to drop for the space of about two months, commencing at the same season as the apricots. The Arabs declare that it falls only by night, and that if there be a moon the supply is more plentiful. If a goat approach the tree, the manna is said to dry up and disappear. The grove of tamarisks called Tarfat el Gidarain, in Wády es Sheikh, yields the most plentiful harvest of manna to the Arabs. Except in name, the manna of Sinai bears no resemblance whatever to the miraculous food described in Exodus. While on this subject, I cannot help alluding to the attempts made by Burckhardt and others to identify the *gharkad*, a plant yielding a sweet red berry, with the "tree" used by Moses to sweeten the waters at Marah. It is certain that the gharkad neither has nor is supposed to have any such properties; but it may be not uninteresting to remark that the word "tree" (*shejer*) in the Bedawín dialect is simply synonymous with a drug or medicament of any kind.

The observations upon the extreme poverty of the Bedawín of course apply only to the Towarah inhabiting the barren mountain districts of Sinai; the Arabs of some parts of Syria, and of the fertile regions of Yemen, Hadhramaut, &c., are often even rich, some of their Sheikhs possessing thousands of camels and horses, as well as immense flocks and herds. In Sinai, however, the Sheikh who possesses three or four camels is regarded as a perfect Crœsus. But poor as they are, some of them, especially the Garrásheh, possess negro slaves who look after the camels and do some of the harder menial work. They are treated with kindness by their masters, who do not regard them at all as inferior beings, though they are of course excluded from the right of intermarriage. The Towarah are a hardy, well-made race, and the men, though clad in the most wretched tatters, have often a certain air of dignity about them. Their dress consists of a white shirt, with long open sleeves (which serve as receptacles for their smaller valuables), fastened round the waist with a leathern girdle, and over this is worn the *'abba* or long robe of goat's or camel's hair. They seldom wear the kefîyeh, or gaily striped head-dress with which we are familiar in pictures of the Bedawín, but prefer the turban and the fez. Sandals made of "fish skin" or rather the hide of a species of Dugong, obtained from the Red Sea near Sherm, are also worn by the men.

The women are all closely veiled, wearing what Thackeray has aptly and graphically described as a "nose-bag." They tattoo their chins, and the married women plait their hair into a kind of knot or horn in front, which is frequently surmounted by a red bead, and seldom if ever untied; the unmarried girls dress their hair in short curls over the forehead, across which they tie an ornament called a *Shebeikeh*, made of red cloth with pendants of mother-of-pearl. A loose blue frock, a string of beads, pieces of bright metal, glass, &c., and a large blue mantle over all, complete their costume.

The children are for the most part without clothing of any kind, though in the cold weather they are sometimes furnished with a piece of goatskin, or a tattered strip torn from a worn-out 'abba and turned whichever way the wind blows. The scanty food and constant exposure produce, as might be expected, many diseases, especially amongst the aged persons and children; and intermittent fever, ague, asthma, and neuralgia, are by no means uncommon. The Towarah, too, are sometimes visited by an epidemic, probably the plague, which they call *el waj' el asfar* "the yellow pest." It comes with the hot winds and strikes men down suddenly in the midst of their occupations, but it is said never to attack "the country of our Lord Moses, where grow the *Shiah* and Myrrh;" that is, the elevated granite region about Jebel Músa.

The Arabs have an idea that every Frank is an adept in the science of medicine, and we were incessantly besieged by swarthy Bedawín afflicted with every ill that human flesh is heir to. When their malady was of a simple nature, we gave them some harmless remedy from our medicine chest, often with beneficial results; but sometimes our skill was severely taxed. I remember an old Arab coming to me one day for medicine for his eyes. He had been afflicted with partial blindness from his birth, and insisted, in spite of my protestations, that I could cure him if I would. As I could get rid of him in no other way, I gave him a seidlitz-powder, and some pomatum to rub over his eyes. He received the nostrums with expressions of the most fervent gratitude, and asked whether the efficacy of the prescription would be marred by his taking a little coffee. In the morning he returned to tell me that he could see better than he had been able to do for twenty years.

With all their sufferings and privations, the Towarah seem happy and contented, and as their own proverb has it:

"A maghrabí (Morocco) sword, a pretty wife, a handsome dromedary; whoso possesses these three things, his heart is glad."

The Bedawín of Sinai, on their own reckoning, number about 4000 males; for an Arab never counts the females or younger boys of his family in a census of the tribe. They are spoken of collectively as the Towarah (singular Túrí), or Arabs of Tor, the ancient name of the Sinaitic Peninsula. They are not the aboriginal inhabitants of the place, but came over with the Mohammedan conquests, and their predecessors seem to have been a branch of the Aramæan race, the same with the Midianites spoken of by Macrizí, and the Saracens of early European historians. If any descendants of these still remain, they must be sought for amongst the Jibálíyeh tribe, whose name, "Mountaineers," would seem to imply a closer relationship with the soil.

Each tribe has three sheikhs; the office is hereditary, descending in a direct line from father to son. The sheikh is rather an agent and arbitrator than a ruler, his only duties being to collect and stipulate for the hire of camels, to represent his tribe in any dealings with the government, and to settle disputes among the Bedawín themselves. For the first the sheikh receives a small commission. The method of recovering a debt is as follows: when an Arab has a claim against another, and payment is refused, he comes before the chief sheikh of his tribe and deposits as a pledge a knife, a gun, a camel or other property, according to the importance and amount of his claim, and this pledge is called *rizgah*. The defendant is obliged to make a similar deposit, and the plaintiff, in case of his refusal, is empowered to obtain it from him by force or stratagem. Both parties then plead their cause before the sheikh, and should the debt be proved the debtor forfeits his pledge, and can only reclaim it by paying in full the sum at issue. An appeal may be made against the decision of the first sheikh to the other two, but in each case a fresh deposit must be made, and the loser of the suit may possibly thus forfeit all three of his pledges, and after all be compelled to pay the original sum demanded. As a rule the decisions of the sheikhs are just and impartial, but instances of "eating bribes" are not absolutely unknown, at least amongst the Towarah.

In case of theft, the owner assesses the value of the stolen property, and the sheikh steps in to enable the litigants to effect a compromise or equitable arrangement. When a fair price or amount of compensation has once been fixed, the person robbed may take and sell any of the thief's possessions to the same amount, in case of the latter refusing to pay. Theft is of such rare occurrence that it is treated as a mere civil transaction.

The 'Agyd is a military officer, who in time of war takes the command of the whole Towarah forces. His authority only extends to actual military operations, and in time of peace he is regarded merely as a private individual. This office is hereditary in the Sawáliheh tribe and is at present held by their head sheikh, Fatíh.

The Bedawín have no criminal code, properly so called, except in the case of murder, and then the law of the blood-feud is rigidly enforced, the nearest male relative of the slain killing the murderer at the first opportunity. But even here a pecuniary compensation may be made and accepted, although it is generally fixed at too high a sum to come within a Túri's limited means.

The Sawáliheh and Jibalíyeh punish adultery with death, the seducer being shot by the injured husband or his relatives, as in the case of a blood-feud for homicide, whenever and wherever he may be found. The Emzeineh and Teyáhah do not however enforce this blood revenge for seduction, but accept a sum of money or a number of camels, the amount of damages being assessed by an arbitrator as in an ordinary civil dispute.

The ceremony of marriage amongst the Bedawín of Sinai is thus conducted: the intending bridegroom with five or six friends calls upon the father of the girl, who prepares and sets before them a bowl of food and some coffee, and when they have partaken of the refreshments the bridegroom opens the conversation by expressing a desire for a more intimate relationship with the family. "Welcome," replies the father; "and I in my turn require a thousand piastres of you as a dowry." After a great deal of noisy discussion he consents to an abatement of 500 or 600 piastres of the sum, and the bargain is concluded. This is the signal for great rejoicings, and the young men of the party amuse themselves with various games and trials of skill, shooting at an ibex-head set over the tent-door as a mark being one of the most favourite pastimes. The Khatíb or public notary of the tribe is then called in; he takes a piece of the herb called gassáleh and wraps it up in the turban of the intending bridegroom. Taking then both their hands in his own, he places the folded turban between them, and, pressing them closely together, addresses the father of the bride: "Are you willing to give your daughter in marriage to such an one?" to which he replies, "I am." The bridegroom is also asked: "Do you take the girl to wife for better or worse?" On his replying, "I do take her," the Khatíb says, "If you ill-treat her, or stint her in food or raiment, the sin be on your own neck." The questions and answers are repeated three times, and the betrothal is then considered completed. The girl herself is kept until this time in ignorance of the transaction, and, should she get an inkling of it, it is considered etiquette for her to make a show of escaping to the mountains. When she returns in the evening from tending the flocks and sits down in her father's tent, they place incense on some lighted embers behind her, and fumigate her surreptitiously as a protection against the evil eye. At this moment the Khatíb comes stealthily behind her with the bridegroom's 'abba (or mantle) in his hand, which he suddenly throws over her, exclaiming: "The name of God be with thee! none shall take thee but 'such an one,'" naming her intended husband. Thereupon the girl starts up and tries to escape, calling upon her father and mother for help, with loud cries and shrieks, but she is seized by the women who have collected round her while they repeat the Khatíb's words in noisy chorus, and utter the shrill cries called *zagharit*. A tent is next erected for her in front of her father's habitation, to which she is conducted and then sprinkled with the blood of a sheep sacrificed for the occasion. Here she remains for three days, at the end of which she is conducted by a procession of women to "a spring of living water" (that is, a perennial spring), and after performing her ablutions is led home to the house of her husband, who makes a great feast in her honour. The neighbours also sacrifice a sheep as a contribution to the entertainment, and receive, as well as the women who have assisted at the ceremony, a trifling present in money from the father of the bride. The Emzeineh are the only tribe who depart in any degree from these observances, and with them the girl runs off to hide in the mountains for three days, instead of remaining in a tent near her father. The passion of love is not unknown amongst the Arabs of the desert. The greater freedom enjoyed by the Bedawí girl as compared with the close seclusion of harem life in the towns, and the unrestrained intercourse of the sexes, especially during the great national festivals at the tombs of their saints, often engender such attachments. When a girl who has thus bestowed her affections on the man of her choice is compelled by her friends to espouse another, she takes advantage of the three days' grace allowed her, to escape to the tents of some of the neighbours, and throwing herself on their protection refuses to leave until the unwelcome suitor has relinquished his claims, and an arrangement has been entered into between her lover and her relatives. The story of Jebel el Benát, "the Girls' mount," presents an interesting instance of these romantic attachments; two girls who were to be married to men they did not like, escaped to the mountains and perished of hunger, rather than prove faithless to their lovers. Burckhardt says they twisted their hair together and precipitated themselves from the cliffs, but this part of the story is now forgotten in Sinai. As soon as a child is born, the mother places it in a hole made in the ground, called *girbás;* she then proceeds to swathe it in cloth or linen, bandaging it from the knees to the loins, after which it is slipped into a cradle, or rather bag, called *zangád*, and its eyes and eyebrows are ornamented with *kohl*. Its head is then pressed into proper shape and tightly bandaged up; a piece of perfumed gum placed in its hand, and bracelets of beads, and of small copper coins called *nuss*, fastened upon its arms and legs, complete the infant's toilette, which is renewed night and morning only.

After childbirth the woman remains seven days in the house, and some even prolong this period to forty days. On the seventh day her clothes are all scrupulously washed, and if the child be a boy a feast is made in its honour, but for a female child no festivities are observed; for, say the Bedawín, *el benát battáleh*, "girls are good for nothing." This dislike of female children was carried to a frightful extent by the Pre-Islamitic Arabs, and the abolition of the practice of burying their daughters alive, *wad el benát*, as it was called, was among the most striking and salutary of the reforms introduced by Mohammed.

The rite of circumcision, as practised among the Bedawín, is attended with great festivities and rejoicing.

On the eve of the appointed day they erect a tent, which is decorated and carpeted in readiness for the morrow's ceremony. When the morning comes, all who can afford it bring a lamb or some other contribution towards the feast, and proceedings are commenced with a public breakfast. At noon, another sheep called '*ágireh* is sacrificed, the tendons of its right heel being previously cut, whence the name, which signifies "hamstrung." The children to be operated on are then seated in a circle upon the carpet within the tent, and a curtain is hung before the door. They are next ceremoniously washed by their mothers, care being taken that their feet shall not touch the bare ground until the operation is complete. Each child is then decked out in all its mother's beads and ornaments, a knife is placed in one hand, and a wooden cross decorated with coloured rags into the other, and in this condition they are carried out and placed upon the shoulders of the men. A procession is thus formed, headed by men holding pans of burning incense, firing off pistols and beating sticks together, and makes the circuit of the tent three times.

The mothers of the children, before leaving the tent proceed to wash their feet in the large bowl previously made use of for the children, each holding a hand-mill balanced on her head all the time, after which they join the procession. When these preliminaries are concluded and the children re-arranged around the tent, the operator proceeds with his duties, first asking permission of the father of each child in turn, and demanding exemption from all penalties in case of a dangerous or fatal result. He then receives a small fee for each of the children operated on. After circumcision the boy is not allowed again to enter the women's apartments. The day's festivities conclude with a grand *fantasia*, and a goat's head is generally set up as a mark for the young hunters of the tribe to shoot at, a leg or shoulder of the animal being given to the successful competitor.

When a Bedawí dies, the corpse is at once taken out of the tent to a convenient place, washed with soap-and-water and shrouded. A bag containing a little corn (called a *shehádeh*) is placed beside it, and it is immediately buried. As soon as it is placed in the grave, the friends of the deceased beat upon the ground with a stick, recite the Fátihah and cry out: "Oh, Thou most compassionate! have mercy upon us, oh, gracious God." They then tap with a small pickaxe at the head of the grave and address the deceased in these words: "When the twain Green Angels[*] shall question and examine thee, say, 'The feaster makes merry, the wolf prowls, and man's lot is still the same, but I have done with all these things. The sidr-tree is thy aunt, and the palm-tree thy mother.'" Each one then throws a little earth into the grave, exclaiming as he does so, "God have mercy upon thee," and the party adjourns to a feast in the tents of the deceased. Another entertainment is given in honour of his memory after the lapse of four months. When a death occurs in an encampment, the women of the family at once go outside the tents; and, taking off their head-dresses, commence a loud and impassioned wailing, which they continue throughout the day.

It has been the fashion with people who do not understand the Bedawín character to describe them

---

[*] Nakír and Munkir; see Sale's Koran, Prel. Discourse, Sect. iv.

as an irreligious and profane race, but this is by no means correct. It is true they do not often perform the ostentatious Mohammedan ceremonial worship, but I have frequently seen our Arab guides grow silent and contemplative towards sunset as they walked along with their camels, and on riding up to them have overheard the following simple prayer: "Oh Lord, be gracious unto us! In all that we hear or see, in all that we say or do, be gracious unto us! Have mercy upon our friends who have passed away before us. I ask pardon of the Great God. I ask pardon at the sunset, when every sinner turns to Him. Now and for ever, I ask pardon of God. Oh Lord, cover us from our sins, guard our children and protect our weaker friends!" At sunrise they say: "I seek refuge with the Great God from Satan accursed with stones*. Deliver me from evil, provide for me and for my brethren the faithful. Oh Lord, be gracious unto us! for a people that prospers is better than a people that strives. Oh Lord, uncover not our inmost faults, protect our children and our weaker friends. Oh Lord, provide for me, thou who providest even for the blind hyena!" Before sleep the Bedawí says: "I lay down my head to rest, and the Lord is my security against remote evil and against present harm." They preface every prayer with the words: "I desire to pray, and I seek guidance from God; for good and pure

---

* Er Rajím, *i.e.* "pelted." The Angels are said to pelt the genii and devils with stones to prevent them from eaves-dropping at the gate of heaven. It is thus the Arabs account for the phenomena of shooting-stars.

prayers come from God alone. Peace be upon our Lord Abraham and our Lord Mohammed."

They believe that, when a man rises up from sleep in the morning, the spirit of God sits upon his right shoulder and the devil on his left. A Túri Arab therefore, on waking, invariably repeats the exorcising formula : " I seek refuge in God from Satan accursed with stones," sprinkling himself, when possible, with water as he utters the words. Without this precaution they believe that the good spirit would take flight and the evil one remain with them throughout the day. At sunset the same ceremony is repeated. Professedly the Bedawín are Mohammedans, but few of them know anything more of that religion than the name. They have many gross and absurd superstitions, but deprived as they are of all instruction and cut off from all civilisation, this is not to be wondered at. Their ideas upon the creation and resurrection are curious; they say : " In the beginning God created man, and when He had made him, He turned him not adrift, but created also for his use the camel and the ass, the sheep, the goat and the ibex which is in the mountains. And the Lord taught him to sow and reap and to milk camels, and gave him moreover the axe wherewith he might fell the trees. And the Lord made small birds when he was wroth with man, to eat up the seed which he had sown and spoil the young crops and the fruit, that man might be humbled from his pride. Then God made the serpent; he made it deaf one month and blind one month alternately, that it should not harm mankind. But when man forgets his Maker then the serpent stings him. Times and seasons too did God create for the service of man; and if the Lord wills it man prospers, but when He wills it he can make him poor indeed." "At the end of the world," say they, "there will be a general resurrection, and on that day the world will melt. Then those who have done good and those who have done evil shall rise together from their tombs; the good shall rise with their hands above their heads, and the wicked with their arms close down by their sides. Then there shall come a dreadful flight of vultures to assail them, and the good, having their hands free, shall repel their attacks and receive no harm, but the wicked will remain helpless until their eyes are all pecked out." The Arabs still practise the rite of sacrifice at the tombs of their saints, as well as at certain other spots, such as the summit of Jebel Músa, to which some peculiar sanctity is believed to attach.

Like most untutored people, the Bedawín have a profound belief in the efficacy of charms and philters, which are generally prepared from birds and animals; the Rakhameh, or Egyptian vulture, furnishes a favourite charm which is thus prepared: take the body of a vulture "tinted by the hand of the prophet's daughter," *i.e.*, with a variegated breast, and bury it in the ground for forty days. At the expiration of that period put it into a pot and boil until all the flesh has disappeared. Next, take the first white bone that sticks up from amongst the others in the pot, and retire with it to some secluded spot, where neither men nor dogs are likely to approach. The evil spirits will then appear and seek to terrify the operator, but if he have a stout heart they will take flight, and other genii will appear, who will reveal to him many wonderful and useful secrets of nature. This bone too is supposed to be an efficacious love-charm, nothing more being required than to rub it upon the dress of a girl to secure her affections at once. The owl and the hyena are also used as charms, and the burnt feathers of the former, and the boiled flesh of the latter, are considered as infallible specifics for numerous disorders. They have many strange superstitions respecting animals; the coney, for instance, is said to be "man's brother," and they point to the peculiar conformation of its hands, feet, &c., in proof that it is the descendant of a human being transformed; they will not eat its flesh, and declare that if a man were to do so, he would never look upon his mother or father again. The leopard and *hudhud* are also supposed to have been originally human beings. The last named is not the hoopoe, (called also *hudhud* in Arabic,) but a mysterious bird which may be heard in the mountains uttering a cry that resembles its name; the Bedawín declare that no one has ever seen it, and they looked upon our attempts to discover the creature, that was often screaming out its monotonous note apparently within a few yards of us, as both impious and futile.

We were unable to discover a specimen, but conjectured it to be a species of owl. There is also a quaint notion prevalent throughout the desert with regard to snakes, which, the Arabs say, may occasionally be seen fighting for the possession of a bead or precious stone. If the combatants can be killed, and the stone found, the lucky owner will be protected from the bites and stings of all venomous reptiles, so long as he keeps it about his person. There are no professional snake-charmers amongst the Towarah, as in Egypt, Morocco and elsewhere, but every tribe has an official called the Háwí, who is supposed to be venom-proof, and to have the power of staunching wounds and curing hurts by his breath. The necessary qualification for this office is that his mother, before he has tasted any other solid food, should cause him to swallow a cake composed of seven barley-corns, seven grains of wheat, a small scorpion, and a hornet, all pounded and mixed together.

Old Sálem ibn Husein, the chief guide of the expedition, professed to have become a Háwi, but we observed that when we encountered a really venomous snake, he put but little faith in his own powers and preferred stoning it from a safe distance.

The Towarah are entirely free from the lawless, predatory instincts which distinguish other Bedawín tribes. Their isolated position, the inaccessible nature of their mountains which have for ages protected them from hostile incursions, and the immediate influence of a settled government, have all contributed to make the Arabs of Sinai an exception to the curse pronounced against Ishmael, "his hand will be against every man, and every man's hand against him." (Gen. xvi. 12.)

CHAPTER VI.

MOUNT SINAI.

Camp at Jebel Músa. Sálem and the hyena. Ascent of Mount Sinai. The Pilgrims' Road; Moses' Fount; Chapel of the Œconomos; Legend of Our Lady of the Fleas. The Confessional Archway. Chapel of Elijah; the cypress. Summit of Mount Sinai. The Delivery of the Law. Rás Sufsáfeh and the Plain of Er Ráhah. Continuation of Pilgrims' Road. The Convent of the Forty Martyrs. The Rock in Horeb. The Mould of the Golden Calf.

HAVING paid our introductory visit to the monks, we proceeded to fix upon a site for our camp, a question of some importance, as we were to stay at Jebel Músa six or eight weeks. The spot selected was a pleasant, sheltered one, lying in a slight depression at the foot of Aaron's Hill. True, we were given to understand that the place was infested by hyenas, but this only added to the romance and excitement of the thing. Wonderful stories the Arabs told us of the cunning of these beasts: how, for instance, a hunter lay down to sleep with his dog and powder-flask beside him, when the hyena, of whom he was in quest, seized the opportunity and the dog, devoured the latter, and walked off with the powder-flask, without arousing the hunter from his sleep. One hyena, attracted by the savoury odours of the cook's tent, did visit us for several successive nights, carefully selecting a moment when dinner or sleep was engrossing all our energies, and consequently always skulking off before any one could snatch up a gun. Emboldened by long impunity, he ventured into the small tent in which the stores were kept, and at last appeared before the astonished gaze of our two Arab "helps" who had sought shelter there. Sálem, one of the Arabs aforesaid, and our own most trusty guide, determined to revenge himself on the intruder, and having borrowed a gun, sat up the following night in hopes of getting a shot at the foe. About midnight an echoing report startled the camp, and rushing out we met old Sálem, who in a triumphant whisper declared that he had done the deed. Following him in an excited procession, we beheld, stretched before the door of the tent, the mangled remains of an Arab cur! To this day the word *dhabá‘* (hyena) is an abomination to Sálem's ears, and if applied to an animal of the canine species it reduces that intelligent Bedawí to the temporary condition of a drivelling idiot. This reminds me of another incident of which he was the hero. One night, during the operation of "flashing the base"—that is, of ascertaining the direction of the base-line with reference to the true north, as indicated by the culmination of the pole-star—old Sálem was set to watch over the safety of an altitude-and-azimuth instrument. As he sat at his lonely post, his imagination peopled the darkness around him with all sorts of undefined horrors, and on our return he declared that he had heard the devil himself uttering an awful shriek. While he spoke, a well-known sound issued from a neighbouring rock, and Mr Holland making for the spot, brought down a fine white owl, the cause of Sálem's alarm. Thinking to laugh him out of his superstition, we held the bird up before him, and told him that was his fiend. An English peasant youth, under somewhat similar circumstances, wept that he had shot a cherubim, but Sálem regarded the corpse with a resigned air and merely said sententiously, "Ah! just as I expected. That's one of his tricks."

Camp life in these latitudes is the most healthful, enjoyable thing possible, but it has its vicissitudes too. One must expect now and then to find one's self buried amid the *débris* of an uprooted tent, to behold one's dinner hopelessly mixed up with sand, which a sudden storm brings on, or to be obliged to turn out barefoot in the cold and rain to slacken the tent ropes. A whirlwind is the most curious of all the visitations to which one is exposed; it is as violent as the most awful storm, tearing up every thing in its path, but it is so partial that you may stand a yard or so off and watch its progress undisturbed. When, as once happened to me, it is your neighbour's tent which is blown about his ears while your own canvas is motionless, there is a great satisfaction to be derived from witnessing this strange atmospheric phenomenon. Such little casualties, however productive of indigestion and rheumatism they might be in our northern climes, are rather amusing than otherwise in desert life, but like most luxuries they must be enjoyed in moderation, or they are apt to pall upon the taste.

Having established our camp, the survey was begun in right earnest, and as soon as the preliminaries could be completed, the work of taking observations commenced. This necessitated passing at least one night upon the summit of Jebel Músa, and as the ascent of this mountain is the first aim and object of the Sinai traveller, I will describe it here more fully. The monks have grouped around their convent all the sacred places mentioned in the Exodus, in order to bring them within a convenient walking distance for the poor Russian pilgrims to whom they have to play cicerone. The route taken by the latter will therefore afford me the best opportunity for detailing the various stations of the ascent in consecutive order.

A rough flight of steps up the deep ravine behind the convent leads to a little recess in the rocks where there is a cool and limpid spring. The Arabs say that this is the identical fountain at which Moses watered the flocks of his father-in-law Jethro, but the monks only venerate it as the hermitage of a cobbler saint. Some way farther up the ravine is a Chapel dedicated to the Virgin of the

Œconomos, of the foundation of which they tell the following story: —

Once upon a time the supplies from Egypt failed, and our monks had nothing to eat. But famine was nothing to the plague of fleas which infested the convent; these made it quite uninhabitable from their numbers and size, and the brethren at last determined to forsake the place, and seek their fortunes elsewhere. Before leaving, however, they marched in solemn procession up these very steps to perform a last pilgrimage to the summit of Mount Sinai. The Œconomos, or Bursar, remained behind to lock the doors, and as he was hastening up to rejoin his companions, he beheld the Virgin Mary, with her Child, seated upon a rock. She bade them return, and promised to help them out of their difficulties. On coming back to the convent, they found a hundred camels laden with provisions and not one of their tiny persecutors left. Since that time, said my informant, such a thing as a flea has never been seen within the convent walls.

But they have been *felt*, as I can testify.

At this point the road crosses to the other side of the ravine, at the top of which you catch the first sight of the splendid cypress by the chapel of Elijah. A few steps farther up is a small archway, at the gate of which St Stephen, the dead porter of the crypt, sat in olden time, to shrive pilgrims and give them, if found worthy, a certificate to the friar who guarded the second gate, higher up. By him they were again subjected to an examination and, that ordeal passed, they were allowed at length to tread upon the sacred summit of Sinai*. Near this gate is a natural trough in the rock, wherein the rain-water collected and served for the hermit's use. On the second of the two gates is a Greek inscription, but it is now so weather-worn as to be quite illegible. Passing beneath these two arches we come upon a large basin, in the midst of which stands a little building containing two chapels, one dedicated to Elijah and the other to Elisha. On the right hand of the altar in the inner chapel is a grotto, said to be the identical cave in which the prophet dwelt during his sojourn in Sinai. Both chapels are now dismantled, and, with the exception of a rude stone altar, and the remnants of a fresco here and there, no other decorations remain but the scribbled names of travellers and pilgrims. Your true "tourist," be he from London, New York or St Petersburg, is eminently exclusive, and though he cannot claim for himself the sole right of visiting every interesting spot and thenceforth closing it against the world, he is determined that no one shall follow him without learning that he John Smith could also afford to

---

* Here, an old traveller tells us, "Many confessionary priests used formerly to sit to hear the confessions of the pilgrims that came to visit these places, and were not permitted to proceed any further, till they had received remission of their sins; so that being made clean by the participation of this sacrament they might obtain a benediction from the Lord and mercy from God our Saviour, repeating as they went the third verse of the xxivth Psalm, 'Who shall ascend into the hill of the Lord? and who shall stand in his holy place? Even he who hath clean hands, and a pure heart, &c.'" *Journal from Grand Cairo to Mount Sinai by the Prefetto of Egypt* (1722).

make the perilous and expensive journey. If the spot be one where he is expected to feel some holy emotions he writes up *laus Deo* after his patronymic, and thus conceals his snobbish ostentation with a little cheap piety and brummagem enthusiasm. Muslim visitors are no less devout and have blazoned forth upon the walls their conviction that Heaven has brought them there to testify that "there is no god but God and that Mohammed &c.;" though what they could find in this dirty, dilapidated den to confirm their belief in Mohammed's prophetic office is more than I have yet been able to discover. The whole of this part of the mountain is called by the monks the Mount of Elias.

A flight of steps, like those at the commencement of the ascent, leads up to the summit, but before reaching this we come to a small plateau on which is the mysterious camel's foot-print which I noticed in a previous chapter. Our own ascent, on the occasion to which I have just alluded, was made in the morning, and at sunset we sought refuge for the night in the deserted shrine of Elijah, where we dined and made our beds.

Like most other monkish institutions, our lodging was romantic but dirty, and the scene which I contemplated from between my blankets seemed to take me back to mediæval times. A *fānūs*, or paper lantern, shed an uncertain ray over the recumbent figures of our own party, and threw the rest of the quaint old chapel into deeper shade, in the midst of which sat our Syrian servant;

his bright coloured attire absorbed nearly all the light of a candle which he held in his hand, leaving only just sufficient to reveal the wild form of an unkempt Greek monk reclining on a bed of rushes behind him.

The next morning we saw the sunrise from the summit of Sinai, a sight which few of us will, I think, ever forget. The effects were, if possible, more beautiful than those of sunset, and a few clouds which still lingered around the peaks heightened and concentrated the lovely colouring of blue and gold and rosy light.

VIEW FROM THE SUMMIT OF SINAI.

The view from the summit does not embrace so comprehensive a prospect of the Peninsula as that from the more commanding peaks of Katarína.

or Serbâl; but the wild desolation of those majestic crags, solitary ravines, and winding valleys, added to the solemn and sacred associations of the scene, cannot fail to impress the beholder with wonder and awe. Yet the desolation of Horeb does not oppress the soul, for in the clear sky, the pure air, and the unbroken stillness of the ancient rocks and labyrinthine valleys, there lurks the "still small voice" that tells us of a present God. One thing alone—a storm—could enhance the sublimity of such a scene; and what a storm was that when there were "thunders and lightnings and a thick cloud upon the mount—and mount Sinai was altogether on a smoke because the Lord descended upon it in fire, and the smoke thereof ascended as the smoke of a furnace and the whole mount quaked greatly." (Exod. xix. 16, 18.) No wonder then, that "all the people that was in the camp trembled." The most striking view of all is that obtained from the Râs Sufsâfeh, the bluff at "the nether end of the mount." Passing through a narrow glen and across a wide basin, you come to a little chapel dedicated to the "Holy Zone of the Virgin Mary," beside which grows a scanty willow-tree, or rather osier, which gives the name (Sufsâfeh) to this portion of the block. To the left of this is a ravine, a stiff climb up which will lead you to the cleft. Here the full size of the enormous plain is even more forcibly realised than from below, the mountains standing out like monstrous walls to fence it in on either side, and the Nagb Hawa, or "Pass of the Wind," with the desolate hills beyond, forming an appropriate background to the whole.

VIEW FROM THE CLEFT ON RAS SUFSAFEH.

The summit of Jebel Músa is occupied by a chapel and a mosque, standing within a few feet of each other. They are built of hewn blocks of red granite, the material of the original edifice, which the Arabs are said to have destroyed. Many similar blocks have also been used in constructing the flight of steps which leads up the mountain. The chapel possesses nothing of interest beyond its position, its decorations being of the ordinary tawdry kind in use in the Greek Church. At the north-east corner, outside the building, is a rock, containing a grotto sufficiently large to admit of a person creeping into it; the upper side is indented with a mark something like the impression of a man's hand and head. Here, the monks say that Moses hid himself while he received the Law; and into this, say the Arabs, he crept, in obedience to the Divine command, when the Lord spake to him, saying, "Creep thou in, O Moses, for thou canst not bear my glory."

The mosque is a square building, and has now fallen entirely out of repair; the *mihráb* (or niche indicating the direction of Mecca) and the various scrawls of Arab pilgrims being all that is left to indicate the nature of the place. In the rock which serves as the foundation is a small cave with a *mihráb*, and a flight of six or eight steps leading down into it. This is said to have been the resting-place of Moses during the forty days of his sojourn upon the mount.

Before entering upon the question of the exact scene of the delivery of the Law, it will be necessary for me to explain what is meant by the summit of Sinai. Jebel Músa is not a single peak, but a huge mountain block, about two miles in length, and one mile in breadth, with a narrow valley on either side, a somewhat larger one at the south-eastern extremity, and a spacious plain at the north-eastern end. A well watered basin or plateau occupies the centre and this is surrounded by numerous peaks of which two only, those at the extremities, are prominent in height or position. The valley to the south-east is called Wády Seba'íyeh, and above this rises a sheer precipitous mass, which, from its being the highest point in the block, is generally regarded as the true Sinai, the summit of the mountain.

But, imposing and grand as the spot undoubtedly is, a single glance at the valley beneath is sufficient to show that it is not in any way adapted for the encampment of so large a host as that of the Children of Israel, nor for the battle of Rephidim; for the monks most inconsistently place the scene of the encounter with the Amalekites and the reception of the Law in one and the same spot. The summit itself is, moreover, invisible from any part of the spacious plain of Er Ráhah, situated at the other end of the block, but there the mountain terminates in a magnificent bluff, called the Rás Sufsáfeh, which fronts the plain and commands a view of its entire extent. This bluff is divided by a deep cleft, to approach which you cross a basin similar to that in which the cypress and chapel of Elijah are situated. At this secluded spot Moses may have separated from the Elders who had accompanied him thus far on his ascent, and it requires but little imagination to believe that from the cleft itself the Ten Commandments were proclaimed. I have already alluded to the traditional evidence in favour of the identification of Jebel Músa with Mount Sinai; I will now endeavour to show how far the physical aspect of the mountain satisfies the requirements of the Sacred Narrative. We must consider Sinai from two points of view: as the mount on which God spake with Moses and

Elijah; and as the mount from which the law was proclaimed to the assembled people of Israel. First then, considered as the mountain on which God spake with Moses. It is clear, from the accounts given in the Bible, that there must have been a secluded tract of ground on the mountain but independent of the summit; for it was after Moses had gone up into Sinai to meditate apart from the people that "the Lord called him up to the top of the mount."

It may be urged that tradition points to the summit itself as the spot on which the Law was delivered, and that no legendary interest whatever attaches to the Rás Sufsáfeh or to the plain at the northern end of the mountain; I do not however think that this is a very formidable objection.

The physical characteristics of the mountain, considered as a whole, satisfy the conditions required, although the tradition by which we are guided to the identification attaches only to a portion; but as that portion is the summit—the grandest and most imposing of all—it could scarcely have been otherwise. Having found our mountain we are not compelled servilely to follow tradition any further, but may exercise our common sense in determining the rest. As there is no other spot but the plain of Er Ráhah upon which the Children of Israel could have all assembled as spectators, and as from this plain the summit of Jebel Músa is invisible, we are compelled to reject the latter as the site of the proclamation of the Law, although it is far from improbable that it was the scene of the delivery. This indeed seems almost implied in the words of the Bible: "And the Lord came down upon mount Sinai, on the top of the mount: and the Lord called Moses up to the top of the mount, and Moses went up." (Exodus xix, 20.) First, there is the awful descent of the Lord in thunder and fire upon the mountain in the sight of the assembled host; then Moses is called up to the secluded summit to receive the words of the Law from God's own mouth, and again he is sent down to proclaim them to the people. The sequence of events is perfectly natural, and in strict accordance with the present topography of the place.

It is clear from the account in Exodus that the camp was within hearing of, though not visible from, the path by which Moses and Joshua came down from the mount. If, therefore, the people were encamped on and in the neighbourhood of the plain, this path was probably at that end of the mountain which is nearest Er Ráhah.

Now there are five paths up Jebel Músa:

1. A camel-track made by the late 'Abbás Pásha, and leading up from the head of the convent valley.

2. A path at the head of Wády Lejá, and leading up from the ruined convent of El Arba'ín.

3. The "steps" behind the convent of St Katharine, by which from time immemorial pilgrims have made the ascent.

4. A ravine leading up from the head of the

small valley, Wády Sh'reich*, on the north-west side.

5. A second ravine called Sikket Shoéib, or Jethro's road, at the north-east corner of the mountain, close by the mouth of Wády ed Deir, and consequently nearest to the plain.

This path emerges into the valley at the foot of the Hill of the Golden Calf, where our own camp was also situated; it was therefore selected by the members of the expedition as the most convenient and quickest road. Often in descending this, while the precipitous sides of the ravine hid the tents from my gaze, have I heard the sound of voices from below, and thought how Joshua had said unto Moses as *he* came down from the mount, "there is a noise of war in the camp."

We have now to consider Sinai with regard to the Proclamation of the Law to the people. It is clear from the Biblical account that it was a prominent, if not an absolutely isolated mountain. Such passages as "and ye came near and stood under the mountain" (Deut. iv, 11), and, "they stood at the nether part" (Ex. xix, 12), point conclusively to the fact that it was what the

---

* One of the peaks in Wády Sh'reich is called Jebel Abu Mahrúreh, "The Thunder Stricken Mountain," a large portion of its summit having been detached by a thunderbolt striking it. It is a noteworthy fact, as affording some slight additional argument in favour of the traditional identity of this locality with the true Mount Sinai, that in the Mohammedan account of Moses' interview with the Almighty on the Mount, it is stated that "the Lord revealed himself to the Mountain, and it shivered into a thousand fragments; and Moses fell senseless on the ground as though a thunder-clap had smitten him."

Apostle describes it to be, "A mount that could be touched." (Heb. xii, 18.) Here, again, the block of Jebel Músa answers in every way to the description: it is so separated from the adjacent mountains by narrow rugged valleys that it would be easy to "set bounds about the mount" (Ex. xix, 23); a cordon across the mouths of Wádies ed Deir and Sh'reich, and a few men posted upon Jebel Moneijáh to keep the pass leading into Wády Seba'íyeh would be sufficient to accomplish this task. The "nether part of the mount," namely, the bluff of Rás Sufsáfeh rises so abruptly from the plain that you may literally stand under it and touch its base. Again, it is clear that at the foot of Sinai there was a plain commanding a view of the mountain from every part, and sufficiently large to admit of the people manœuvring upon it—for them, at one time, to "come near and stand under the mountain," at another, "to remove and stand afar off." It is not necessary to suppose that all the Israelites were actually encamped upon the plain itself, nor do the words of the Bible even imply it; for we are expressly told that "Moses brought the people forth out of the camp to meet with God." (Ex. xix, 17.) They would doubtless spread over a considerable area, and occupy many of the neighbouring glens, valleys and mountain-sides, especially where there was plenty of water and pasturage for their flocks and herds. All that is required is a plain capable of affording standing room for the Israelites as spectators, and

MOUNT SINAI.

the plain of Er Ráhah more than satisfies this condition. A calculation made by Captain Palmer, from the actual measurements taken on the spot, proves that the space extending from the base of the mountain to the watershed or crest of the plain is large enough to have accommodated the entire host of the Israelites, estimated at two million souls, with an allowance of about a square yard for each individual.

The neighbourhood of Jebel Músa is the best watered in the whole peninsula, running streams being found in no less than four of the adjacent valleys.

Josephus, speaking the language of Jewish tradition, tells us that Mount Sinai was "the highest mountain in the country." Now the observations taken by the Survey Expedition have shewn that the highest point in the Peninsula is Jebel Zebír, one of the peaks of Jebel Katarína. The Arabic lexicographers, one and all, interpret this name as meaning "the mountain on which God spake to Moses," deriving it from the word *zabara*, of which the primary signification is to write or engrave. The peak in question is not visible from the plain or any of the valleys beneath, and can therefore have no pretensions to rivalry with Jebel Músa, but the name and tradition would go far towards excluding the other mountains of the Peninsula which have been proposed as the scene of the Law-giving, but which are in a different range of hills; it would thus furnish strong presumptive evidence in favour of localising the true Sinai in this group, of which Jebel Músa forms a part.

The whole southern portion of the mountain is called by the monks Horeb. It is difficult to determine the exact application of this name, as it appears to be used in the Bible with reference both to the mount itself and to the district in which it was situated. From such considerations, as the meaning of the word, Horeb, "ground which has been drained and left dry," and such expressions as "thou stoodest before the Lord thy God in Horeb," "the rock in Horeb," it would rather seem that the whole desert of Sinai was so called, and that the name was subsequently attached to the Mountain.

Antoninus Martyr in his Itinerary applies the name Sinai to the block of Jebel Músa, and that of Horeb to the "Mountain of the Cross," Jebel Salíb, on the opposite side of the valley. But Jebel Salíb is only a peak of Jebel 'Aríbeh, and that word is etymologically identical with Horeb.

The Arabs look with profound veneration upon Jebel Músa. Once in every year they sacrifice a sheep or goat upon it to the Israelitish Lawgiver, and the doorway of the little mosque upon the summit is all stained and blackened with the blood of victims sprinkled "upon the lintel and on the two side posts." When the year has been a fruitful one, they also sacrifice a camel to Aaron, at the hill in the valley below which bears his name. This last ceremony is called the *rikáb*, or "cavalcade." The animal is decked out with gay streamers, each member of the party contributing some rag or strip of cloth for the purpose, and it is then led three times round the monastery, slaughtered, boiled in a hugh pot borrowed from the monks, and eaten. Of the festivities attending these and similar ceremonies I shall speak more fully in a future chapter.

But to return to the description of the topography. Following the road taken by the Russian pilgrims, we descend into Wády Lejá, where there is a monastery, dedicated to the forty martyrs of Cappadocia, and called the Arba'ín. It has now fallen into disuse, and almost into decay, but is surrounded by a magnificent garden and a fine grove of olive-trees. This place is looked upon by the Arabs as peculiarly sacred. They believe that no robbery can be perpetrated there without immediate detection, and that if a man afflicted with any malady whatever were to sleep within its precincts he would experience instant relief. Here the "spirits" are said to hold nightly revel, and celebrate *fantasias* to the sound of sweet music. It is kept in partial repair, and used as a resting-place for the night by pilgrims who have ascended Jebel Músa, and are preparing for the ascent of Katarína on the following day.

About the middle of the garden is a little hermitage and chapel in which the celebrated St Onufrius lived and died. The saint appears to have slept in a pigeon-hole, in a cave entered by a small square doorway, the rest of the opening being built up with loose stones. On the left-hand side, at the mouth of the wády, there is a ruined convent dedicated to the Twelve Apostles; and in the open space a little farther on is shown the site of the rebellion and punishment of Korah, Dathan, and Abiram. In Wády Lejá we find several rocks to which traditional interest attaches, and amongst them the so called Rock in Horeb which Moses struck. There are sundry niches, or fissures, in this stone which are construed by the credulous into twelve mouths, whence they say that water gushed forth to supply the twelve tribes. Monkish legend, founded on a too literal interpretation of a passage in St James, supposes that this rock followed the children of Israel throughout the whole of their wanderings, and continued to furnish them with water—regarding the stone in fact as a tame waterbarrel always on tap.

A little nearer to the mouth of this valley are some rings of stones placed on flat rocks; they have been described by learned travellers as appertaining to some religious rite of the Bedawín, but those who can question the Arabs for themselves will find that they are used for drying tobacco.

The fine mountain at the entrance to Wády Lejá on the west side, at the foot of which stands the ruined convent of the Twelve Apostles, is called Jebel er Rabbeh. Ammonius, an Egyptian monk, writing in the 4th century, speaks of a slaughter of the monks of Sinai by the Saracens, and tells us that "they found thirty-eight corpses, twelve of which were in the monastery of Gethrabbi." This word is almost identical with the common corruption of the name by the Bedawín at the present day, who frequently call the mountain *Jerrabbeh*, and the convent of the Twelve Apostles is undoubtedly the same as that alluded to in the ancient chronicle.

Continuing our way round the foot of Mount Sinai, we come to a curious hole in the rock, which is known as the Mould of the Calf. It requires, however, considerable faith to detect in it a likeness to that or any other animal.

Near the same spot is shown a hole dug in the ground and supposed to mark the spot where the broken Tables of the Law were buried; the Arabs, however, merely regard it as the work of some infatuated treasure-seeker.

But, whatever we may think of the authenticity of some of these traditions, we cannot quite divest ourselves of reverence as we look upon the places to which they are attached. They *are* considered sacred spots, and as such they do serve to recall most vividly the events which they are supposed to commemorate. But the interesting and solemn associations of the place were marred by the mingled indifference and superstition of the monkish crew; and it was only in the solitude of the mountains, or in the retirement of our own camp, that we really felt that we were at Sinai.

CHAPTER VII.

THE NEIGHBOURHOOD OF JEBEL MÚSA.

Rocks with legends. Wády T'láh. Bedawín Camp. Storms; a disaster. Collection of Arab stories. Doctoring the Bedawín. Ascent of Jebel Katarína: the Partridge Fountain; view from the summit. 'Abbás Pasha's Palace. Jebel Moneijáh. Excursion to Jebel Hadíd. Primeval stone Remains. Maghrabí Treasure-Finders. Wády Nasb. Christmas at Sinai.

OUR camp was stationed in the Convent valley for nearly two months, so that we had ample opportunities for making ourselves acquainted with the various objects of interest, traditional and natural, in which the neighbourhood abounds. On the projecting spur of the mountain immediately above our tents was the burial-ground of Sheikh Nahámeh, to whose tomb the sick or decrepit amongst the Arabs resort in great numbers and offer sacrifices; they believe that in life he was a physician, and that he still has the power of healing their various disorders if properly propitiated with blood. A little farther on is a large rock dotted all over with white marks and looking as though it might have served as a target for rifle practice; it is in reality used by the Arabs as a standard for measuring their height, whence its name "the Measuring Stone." In addition to the monkish traditions mentioned in the last chapter, the valleys around Jebel Músa contain several spots to which native legendary interest attaches. In Wády ed Deir, on the right hand side and not far from Aaron's Hill, there is a small boulder covered with "cup markings" such as Scotch antiquaries are familiar with, and which also bears an indentation, the impression, it is said, of Moses' back. "Look," said an Arab to me as I was regarding it one day with curiosity, "look how the Prophet, on whom be peace, has jobbed it with his staff." At the mouth of Wády Lejá, too, there is a rock with a large protuberance on the side; this is called by the Bedawín Hajar el Gidar, "the Pot Rock," and is believed to contain hidden treasure. Every Arab as he passes by taps it with his staff or throws a stone at it, hoping that the mysterious pot will burst open and enrich him with a golden shower. Near the head of the same valley, by which, the Bedawín say, Moses descended from Mount Sinai, they point out the Shagg Músa or "Moses' Cleft;" lower down, also, they shew the Hajar el Magarín, "The Rock of the Conjoined ones," two huge rocks on either side of the narrow footpath, which, like those in Wády Berráh, they believe to have been originally a single mass miraculously split apart to admit of Moses passing through. "When Moses went up into Mount Sinai to speak with God," they say, "the world was subject to his command, mountains cleaved asunder, and hard rocks melted like wax before him." It is a curious superstition, and one by no means confined to the Bedawín, that all holy personages possessed the faculty of leaving their impression on rocks and stones. Perhaps this may in some measure be accounted for, by supposing it to be the result of a vague intuitive perception of geological phenomena, imperfectly understood and therefore referred to the supernatural. The particular case, however, of the rocks in question cleft in twain by Moses in his descent from the Mount, may contain some lingering record of the scene when "Moses' anger waxed hot, and he cast the tables out of his hands, and brake them beneath the mount" (Exod. xxxii, 19).

The nature of our work took us into many an unfrequented nook, and we often lighted on little pieces of mountain landscape of which the ordinary traveller knows nothing. Perhaps the most picturesque and beautiful of these is the Wády T'láh, a valley running parallel with the plain of Er Ráhah, a fertile and well-watered glen, which one would little expect to find in the midst of such utter desolation. Between steep and fantastic rocks you look down a long vista of verdant gardens, and listen to the grateful sound of a brawling stream that dashes along past thickets of fruit-trees, and falls ever and anon over smooth fern-clad boulders. You seem suddenly to have come upon some peaceful vale, such as one sees here and there amidst the mountains of the Apennines, and for a moment you may forget the barren, awful wilderness in the midst of which you stand. But it is only for a moment, and the fact soon forces itself upon you, that the pleasant gardens are after all but vestiges of monastic industry of earlier times; no hand now tends the flowers or prunes the vines, and the very beauty of the scene adds only to the general desolation from the oppressive sense of neglect and desertion which it leaves behind.

In the neighbourhood of Jebel Músa were several encampments of the Bedawín, to whose tents I paid frequent visits. As I approached, the men would rise, and courteously invite me to partake of their repast; the children would roar, the ladies look scandalized, and, especially the old and ugly ones, conceal their features more carefully in their dark blue cloaks, while all in frantic chorus screamed out the word in which an Arab's hopes, aspirations and memories are concentrated—*bakhshish*. On one of these occasions I noticed an old woman weaving at the tent-door. Her loom was a primitive one, consisting only of a few upright sticks upon which the threads were stretched; the transverse threads were inserted laboriously by the fingers, without the assistance of a shuttle, and the whole fabric was pressed close together with a piece of wood. Beside her stood a younger female spinning goats' hair to supply the old lady with the materials necessary for her task. Many such a group as that which we saw before us must there have been in the Israelitish camp when the people brought the "Lord's offering to the work of the tabernacle of the congregation," "and all the women whose hearts stirred them up in wisdom spun goats' hair" (Exod. xxxv, 21, 26).

The weather, though cold, had been hitherto beautifully clear and favourable to the work, but on the morning of the 11th of December a fiercer gale than we had yet experienced began to blow, and a mass of black clouds which came sailing majestically over Er Ráhah portended a coming storm. Nor was the visitation long deferred, for about the middle of the afternoon, as the officers were busily occupied in their computations, a sudden gust of wind arose which loosened every peg of the tent they were sitting in, and without a moment's warning smothered them in a confused heap of canvas, books, and papers. The barometer Captain Palmer had the presence of mind to seize upon at once, and so prevented its being seriously injured. Some valuable papers, however, containing a great part of the calculations of the preceding day, were carried off by the wind before they could be secured, and were lost amidst the intricacies of the neighbouring mountain-paths. Every one of course immediately rushed up to the scene of the disaster, old Sálem, our Arab factotum, being amongst the earliest arrivals. At first the sight seemed to unnerve him;—one officer was fruitlessly struggling to extricate his head from a fold of canvas, another was heroically wrestling with a mountain barometer; while above the general ruin the emancipated sheets of paper were merrily whirling in the air. At last the old man appeared to comprehend the situation: "This," he said phlegmatically, "this is from God;" and taking out his pipe, he sat down upon the ground with an air of resigned composure, and began to smoke. Salvo our cook, however, induced him by the persuasion of a thick stick to exchange his contemplation for action, and assist in setting the tent to rights, a task that was not accomplished for nearly two hours. This was the beginning of the bad weather which ultimately drove us from Jebel Músa to seek the less lofty and consequently more temperate region of Feirân. The gales were soon followed by a snow-storm, and the effect produced by this was one of the finest that I have ever witnessed. As the mist rolled away before the rising sun, great masses of clouds were seen overhanging the plain, the valley faded away into a dim vista of apparently interminable length, while the mountains, now capped with snow, seemed twice their usual height, and here and there, as they caught the morning rays, shone out with prismatic colours that were refracted by the mist into a myriad sparkling points of light.

During my stay at Jebel Músa I endeavoured to make myself acquainted with the thoughts and sentiments of the Towarah, and to gather as much as possible of the folk-lore of the Sinai desert. My usual practice was to devote a portion of every evening to a conversation with the Arabs over their camp-fires, and to take down in their own words the tales and stories which each had to recount. These I tested by subsequent enquiry whenever I reached a spot to which I either knew or supposed a legend to attach, and in this way succeeded in bringing to light many interesting traditions, which are not only undoubtedly native in their origin but even distinct from or antagonistic to the monkish accounts, and which have an important bearing on the history of the Exodus. Such are the Arab traditions in the neighbourhood of Wády Feirán of the rock struck by Moses, the legend of the lost caravan near Hazeroth, and several others, which will be related at full length in their proper place. Where it was possible, I took down these stories in the very words of my Arab informants, and thus succeeded in obtaining a practical insight into the Bedawí idiom, which served me in good stead on many subsequent occasions. Old Sálem was invaluable to me in prosecuting these researches, being one of the greatest authorities of the Peninsula both for legends and topography. I was frequently congratulated by the Bedawín upon having so efficient an ally, who, they assured me, "knew the whole history of the world from beginning to end."

Nothing would convince them that we had not a doctor in the camp; and Holland, having one morning in a playful moment referred some invalided Towarah to me as a great *hakím*, I was forced to accept the greatness thus thrust upon me, and found myself obliged to prescribe for all comers, as the only way of getting rid of their importunities. My first patient was a venerable elder of the tribe, who one afternoon seated himself at the door of the tent, and commenced the usual complaint: *Yá khawájah yújíní galbí,* "My inside pains me, Sir." I was in a decidedly *negligé* costume at the time, but the books and papers that were strewn about the tent, and my long chibouk, gave me a sufficiently learned appearance; I therefore put on a grave air and began to ask him about his malady. I found that he was afflicted with a confirmed asthma of many years' standing, and, as he had cold and bad living to contend with, I did not entertain great hopes of effecting a cure. However, bringing forth a bottle of chlorodyne, I mixed him a dose on the spot, and told him to repeat the Fátihah or opening chapter of the Corán, before swallowing it; for I felt sure that faith and warmth would go some way towards giving him relief. It was quite touching to see the simple trust of that old son of Ishmael, as he set the cup before him, held up the palms of his hands, and repeated the prayer in a fervent tone, all the spectators uttering a solemn "Amen" as he swallowed the mixture, and regarding him for some minutes afterwards with an air of the greatest interest, as though they expected to see him suddenly leap up in all the vigour of restored youth.

We were desirous of leaving for Feirán as soon as possible, but could not do so until observations had been taken from the summit of Jebel Katarína.

We were therefore obliged to brave the weather, and make the ascent.

An hour's walk up the Wády Lejá brought us to the Shagg Músa, "Moses' Cleft," immediately past the convent of the Forty Martyrs, where the actual ascent of the mountain may be said to commence. It is a long but not a difficult climb, though, our first acquaintance with it being made in the midst of snow and ice, it proved rather less agreeable on that than on subsequent occasions. There is not much to interest the traveller on the road, for familiarity will have led him by this time to look on the huge granite precipices, not certainly with contempt, but at least with composure. One pretty spot there is, at the top of the ravine about half way up, a little spring closed in by lofty cliffs, and called the "partridge fountain" (*Máyan es Shinnár*). The monks have a legend that it was miraculously discovered by a partridge flying out therefrom, as their thirsty predecessors bore St Katharine's body from the summit, where it had been mysteriously placed after her decapitation at Alexandria. The Arabs know nothing of this story, and declare that the spring is so named because partridges abound there—so abominably rationalistic are these followers of Mahound. At last you reach the top of the ridge, and step upon a broad plateau, from which rise three immense rounded peaks, the centre one called Jebel Zebír, the most southerly Abu Rumail, and that to the north Katarína. On the last-mentioned peak stands a little chapel dedicated to the saint, and built upon the spot to which the angels are said to have carried her body.

Jebel Katarína had been generally regarded as the highest peak but one in the peninsula, and Umm Shomer as the most elevated point of all; doctors, however, disagreed, and each mountain had many partizans who fiercely supported its claims. The observations taken by the Sinai Expedition have shown that Katarína has the advantage of Umm Shomer by some few feet, and that both are outstripped by Jebel Zebír. Of the three sister peaks, Katarína, Zebír, and Abu Rumail, the first is incomparably the most imposing, consisting of one huge rugged block of porphyry.

For about the first hour of our ascent we got along very well, as the stones which covered the lower portion of the mountain-side were tolerably free from snow; but when we approached the summit our real troubles began. The wind blew bitterly cold, and the road lay over a smooth white expanse of snow, which instead of being firm as it appeared, was a mere trap to let one down knee-deep, amidst sharp slippery stones, imperilling one's limbs at every step. It was a most exasperating walk; our legs had entirely their own way, and one or other of us was constantly disappearing between some concealed boulders, or slipping gracefully down the slope and having to begin again. One of the Arabs flatly refused to go on, but as I insisted, and old Sálem offered to shew him the way, the poor shoeless vagabond started off again with the theodolite on his shoulders. For my part, having slipped back again to my starting-point for the sixth time, I had arrived at the conclusion that life was not worth having under the circumstances, and was about to lie down and perish, when I suddenly caught sight of one of my companions struggling on a little ahead of me. His evidently intense physical suffering cheered me with the thought that I was not alone in my misery; and after a series of startling gymnastics I succeeded in reaching the summit, perfectly exhausted and frozen, and at once lay down to sleep in the snow. In spite of all traditions to the contrary, I awoke in a few minutes much refreshed, and proceeded to enjoy the prospect, which was simply magnificent. To the north-east rises the green summit of Jebel Músa, its colour contrasting strangely with the whitewashed buildings which surmount it; on the right is Jebel ed Deir, and nearer still the great dome-like mass of the Rás Sufsáfeh, beyond which is seen the narrow gorge of the Nagb Hawa. Westward are the graceful peaks of Jebel el Benát and El Jozeh, with the grander range of Serbál and its neighbour Beidhat Umm Tákhah. The foreground of this portion of the landscape is composed of monster masses of rugged granite, which glow like burnished copper in the sunlight. Amongst the forest of peaks may be distinguished a mountain, Jebel Tíníyeh, with a small white edifice upon its highest point. This is the half-finished palace of the late 'Abbás Pasha, Viceroy of Egypt, who carried his

mania for bricks and mortar even into the wilds of
Sinai. Reckless debauchery had begun to tell upon
the Pasha's constitution, and his medical advisers
ordered him to try the desert air. He accordingly
set out with a number of troops, and took up his
quarters at the convent of St Katharine. Feeling
the beneficial effects of the pure mountain air, he
determined to build a palace in the neighbourhood;
and in order to ascertain which was the most
salubrious situation he adopted the following original expedient. Joints of fresh meat were exposed
on all the accessible mountain-tops around, and
that on which the flesh should remain for the long-
est time without corruption was to be declared
the healthiest spot. The choice fell upon Jebel
Tíníyeh; a road to the summit was constructed
with great labour, and the foundations of this
palace laid. But before the building had pro-
gressed very far, his Highness changed his viceregal
mind, and, being influenced by the fables of the
monks, decided to dwell upon the holy mountain
itself, and so enjoy the benefit of Moses' especial
protection, as well as the advantages of the climate.
As a preliminary measure, a road was commenced
over a spur of the northern end of the mountain
at the mouth of the Convent Valley. This again
was abandoned, and the road now known as "the
Pasha's Road" was ultimately constructed at the
south-eastern end of the block, and still forms the
most convenient approach to the summit. Bedawín
tradition furnishes us with the sequel to the

story. "The Pasha," the Arabs say, "went up the mountain by the road which he had himself made. But his heart was full of evil designs, and he wished to desecrate the sanctity of the place. Wherefore our Lord Moses caught him before he reached the summit, and shook him sorely, so that he came down again in a terrible fright, cursed the land and all that were therein, and made the best of his way back to Egypt." Within a few weeks of his return to Cairo, he was murdered by a Mamlouk, whom he had discovered in an intrigue with one of the ladies of his harem; but the unfinished palace stands upon the mountain still, a strange memorial of human fickleness and folly.

The junction of wádies which come down from this point forms a very pleasing feature in the prospect; for, being all lined with well-watered gardens, their verdure softens to some extent the stern and rugged grandeur of the scene. Turning towards the south, the eye wanders over the broad plain of El Gá'ah, with the Gulf of Suez and the shadowy outline of Jebel 'Akrab on the African coast beyond. Next in the mighty panorama come the jagged peaks of Umm Shomer and Jebel eth Thebt; the blue waters of the Arabian gulf, with the hills of the Hejjaz upon its opposite shore; lastly, the bright red mass of Umm 'Alawí, with the sandy labyrinth behind it stretching up to the distant mountains of the Tíh; this seen, you have gazed, without moving from your place, over nearly the whole of the Sinaitic Peninsula.

The view from a mountain in Sinai differs essentially from any other landscape. There is no single ridge over which the sight ranges, or the memory wanders, to fair fields and fertile valleys beyond; it is one mighty prospect of bare and barren peaks, and is bounded only by the desert or the sea. The beauty of the scene, for beautiful it is, is in no way indebted to the accessories of forest or of stream; distance lends no enchantment to the view; the tints are those of sunlight on the coloured stones, the outlines are the natural contours of the rocks.

The descent was almost as fatiguing as the ascent, and we did not reach camp until some time after dark. One of the Arabs knocked up, and had to be left behind with old Sálem, who lighted a fire for him and administered consolation in the shape of tobacco. As they did not appear by the time we had finished our own dinner, we began to get rather anxious, and Holland was even contemplating another journey up the mountain in the dark to take them some food, when they arrived in camp, and soon forgot their fatigues over a tin of soup and a handful of coffee with which we regaled them.

I must not leave my account of the neighbourhood of Mount Sinai without making mention of Jebel Moneijáh, the small conical mountain at the head of the convent valley. In its name, "The Mount of the Conference," there still lingers a traditional reminiscence of that event which gave to this wild and barren region an interest far greater and more human than that possessed by scenes which have witnessed the mightiest struggles in the world's history. It commands a magnificent view of the plain of Er Ráhah, more imposing perhaps than the prospect seen from the Rás Sufsáfeh itself, since the vista is here lengthened by the addition of the convent valley.

THE CONVENT VALLEY FROM JEBEL MONEIJAH.

On the 21st of December it was determined to make an excursion to Jebel Hadíd, for the purpose of investigating the geological features of the district, and especially of examining the ancient tombs and other remains which exist in its vicinity. Jebel Hadíd itself is so called from the quantity of iron ore which is found there in large dykes, often appearing upon the surface of the ground.

So much time had been occupied in getting provision from our store-room at the convent and in packing up, that we did not get off until past eleven o'clock in the morning. Crossing over the pass of Jebel Moneijáh we descended into Wády Seba'íyeh, which many travellers have, with the monks, considered as the scene of Israel's encampment before the mount. Jebel Músa certainly does present an imposing front from this valley, but, grand and rugged as are its precipitous sides, it lacks the marked isolation of the Rás Sufsáfeh, and appears in no way adapted to the events attending the Proclamation of the Law. The name Wády Sebaíyeh is interpreted by most modern travellers "the Keeper's valley," connecting it with *sebá*, "a wild beast," by an etymology suggestive of Wombwell's menagerie, or the Zoological gardens. An allusion is evidently intended to Moses as "the keeper" of Jethro's flocks, but I need hardly say that no such connexion exists, and that the name does not signify the valley of the "Keeper" but rather of the "Brave Youth," an appellation that I should hardly imagine can refer to Moses. The wády itself is a broken uneven valley, inferior even in area to many of its immediate neighbours, and forming a striking contrast to the simple smooth expanse of Er Ráhah. Not to mention other arguments against the identification, it would be simply impossible to "set bounds

SUMMIT OF SINAI FROM JEBEL ED DEIR.

On reaching the watershed, another magnificent landscape bursts upon the gaze, in which the bold outline and clear, delicate colouring of Jebel Nakhleh is the most prominent feature. In most of these valleys the watersheds are very strikingly marked; they are not, as elsewhere, long gradual slopes from a high plateau of land, but are, what their name implies, narrow ridges which, if there were a torrent, would divide its waters and shed them in opposite directions on either side. At half-past four we camped near Jebel Nakhleh, as it was impossible to reach Jebel Hadíd while daylight lasted; but by sunrise the next morning we were up again and on the march. After about five hours' walking along very picturesque valleys with steep sloping sides, we reached our destination, having passed nothing of interest on the road, except a small white cairn set upon a corner rock at the junction of Wádies Rutig and Rahabeh, which was decorated with a few votive tufts of dried grass. The Arabs were not able to tell us anything more about this than that it was called the "Lamplighter's Cairn," and that it had probably been intended as a landmark to guide travellers on their way to the Convent. Jebel Hadíd, the scene of our proposed excavations, is distant a rather long day's journey from the Convent; our camp was pitched in a beautifully sheltered spot, immediately in the neighbourhood of the ancient tombs, and the only drawback to the pleasure of our picnic was that the water, brought from Wády Khasíb some little distance off, was execrable. Although I did not on this occasion assist at the resurrectionist operations, I subsequently visited the spot, and can therefore give some description of the singular remains which exist there.

They resemble the pre-historic remains of Europe and are of two kinds: first, circular houses about ten feet in diameter, built of unhewn stone and covered with a carefully constructed dome-shaped roof, the top of which is closed by a large slab of stone and the haunches are weighted to prevent them from springing out; the entrance is by a low door about two feet wide. They evidently once formed human dwellings, and, in some more perfect ones which we have since examined in another place, bones and charred wood were found in a small cist in the centre which had apparently served as the hearth. They exactly resemble the *bothan* (shielings or beehive huts) of the Shetland Islands, and the chambers discovered in the large cairns at Clava near Inverness. Some few of them had a spiral path running round the outside and were almost identical in their construction with the *talayot*, or so-called ancient watch-towers, found in the Balearic Islands. The second, and seemingly more ancient, kind consists of huge stone circles, some of them measuring a hundred feet in diameter, having a cist in the centre covered with a heap of larger boulders. These are nearly identical in construction with the "Druidical Circles" of Britain. In the cists we found human skeletons, the great antiquity of which was proved not only by the decayed state of the bones, but by the fact that the bodies had in every case been doubled up and buried in such a position that the head and knees met. There are also small open enclosures in the circles, in which burnt earth and charcoal were found. The tombs belonged apparently to a race and age different from that of the round houses mentioned above; of the now silent occupants of the former we have since discovered the deserted dwellings in great numbers in other parts of the country*. These last are of very considerable extent, and quite distinct from the beehive huts; they consist of a collection of circles, enclosed within rudely heaped walls, the stones employed being of precisely the same size and character as those used in the construction of the sepulchral rings and cairns. They were probably the permanent camps of an ancient pastoral people, a conclusion to which we were led by having observed similar enclosures in use at the present day on Mount Hermon. There we noticed low rude walls for penning in the sheep and goats, and into these branches of acacia and other thorny trees were inserted, the whole forming an impassable barrier. Both houses and tombs are called by the Arabs of Sinai *nawâmis* (singular *nâmûs*), or "mosquito houses," their tradition being that the children of Israel built them as a shelter from a plague of mosquitoes which had been sent against them by Heaven as a punishment for their rebellion and sins. Who and what the people were who constructed them it is perhaps impossible now to decide; but one thing seems certain enough, they must have existed in large numbers in the Peninsula, have buried on "high places," and sacrificed at the tombs of the dead. Who can say that it was not on this very blackened earth before us that hungry Israel was tempted to sin, and ate the offerings of the dead?

* At the foot of Jebel el 'Ejmeh, in treating of which locality I shall describe them more fully.

I must confess to a certain ghoul-like propensity for these investigations, and even as I write these lines my hands are begrimed with the dust of defunct Amalekites dug up *three days ago:* for know, O well-washed reader, that I am in the "great and terrible wilderness," and water is at present known to me only as a vehicle for tea.*

An Arab has but one theory as to your intentions in any kind of excavation: you have, of course, come to search for hidden treasure, and your Bedawín guides will always lend a willing hand with the spade or pick-axe, in the hope of coming in for a share of the spoil.

The Maghrabís, or Western Arabs, are the most accredited treasure-finders, and many wonderful tales are told of their mysterious powers. The following story, related to me by Sálem, curiously illustrates this belief. "Some twenty years ago," said he, "there was a girl amongst the Towarah who had intercourse with the other world. Every Friday night the spirits would throw her into convulsions, and crowds of people used to assemble and listen to the prophecies which she uttered on these occasions. Once, when in a trance, she declared that immense treasures lay hidden in the *nawámis* at Jebel Hadíd. Now," continued Sálem, "a year or two back Khawájah Holland came to the Peninsula and dug up some of these very *nawámis* and found skeletons therein. This brought to our minds the words of the prophetess, and my brother Ahmed

---

* The greater part of the present work was written in the Desert.

determined to go to Cairo and consult a Maghrabí. Having found one, he presented him with a few copper coins, but without stating the object of his visit. The 'cunning man,' as usual, burnt some incense, and placing a book in my brother's hands bade him open it wherever his finger might happen to fall. Ahmed did so, and the Maghrabí, having inspected the page, said: 'there is a treasure concealed near the spot where the Khawájah dug into the *námus*,' and offered to accompany him at the expiration of twenty days, to search for it. On the appointed day Ahmed returned, but found the Maghrabí dead."

While the excavations were proceeding, Captain Palmer and I made a surveying excursion down the neighbouring Wády Nasb. This is a beautiful and romantic valley, a grove of *tarfah* trees extending for miles along it, and the rocks on either side being striped with dykes of the most brilliant hues and fantastic patterns. A mile or so up the wády, on the left-hand side, is an aperture in the rocks called Umm Zarabeh, a glance at which will well repay the traveller for a slight deviation from the beaten track. The passage is formed by granite boulders, the smallest of them forty feet square, lying one across the other like so many faggots carelessly thrown down. This leads into an open space, upon the solid floor of which lies an unbroken mass of fallen rock, in size and shape about as large again as the dome of St Paul's Cathedral. At the entrance of the passage is a little spring, modestly oozing out from behind a huge stone, and garnished with some pretty ferns. Farther on, the valley narrows into a magnificent gorge not more than twenty yards across, with sheer precipitous sides some fifteen hundred feet in height. Before leaving the neighbourhood of Jebel Hadíd, Captain Wilson and Mr Holland ascended Jebel Abu Mas'úd for the purpose of making trigonometrical observations as that point was to form the south-eastern limit of the survey.

On our way back to Sinai, we came round Jebel Hadíd into Wády Umm Dhelleh, where we found a number of the more ancient *nawámis*; the stone circles were some of them ninety feet in circumference and composed of boulders from three to five feet long. On a neighbouring hill was a wall constructed with similar stones, and a covered passage, all apparently belonging to the same age. From this we emerged into Wády Wa'ará, a valley which presented the rather remarkable feature of a large smooth terrace or gravel-bank, about two hundred yards wide, and sloping in the same direction as the bed of the wády which ran at a level thirty feet lower on the right-hand side. Presently we struck into our old track, and by sunset were once more in our quarters at Jebel Músa.

We had returned to Sinai in time to spend our Christmas Day there, to celebrate the Advent of Him who was the Fulfilment of the Law beneath the very shadow of the mountain from which the Law was first proclaimed. Christmas morning broke bright and clear; in the desert it was not likely to be ushered in by many extraordinary festivities, but we observed it as a day of rest, and passed it in a very agreeable manner, Mr Holland performing morning service in the mess tent. Nor did we forget the good old customs of the season. True, we had neither holly nor mistletoe, and the nearest approach we could have contrived to a Yule Log would have been to borrow a walking stick from the Œconomos at the Convent; but Salvo, our Maltese cook, had extracted much festivity out of some olive branches and cypress twigs, and the tents were unanimously pronounced to be "most tastefully decorated." And who shall paint the glories of our Christmas dinner of stewed ibex, followed by a real, palpable plum-pudding, made months before by fair hands at home! The *vis inertiæ*, the power of laziness, which followed that meal proved that we did it ample justice.

As our stay at Jebel Músa was drawing to a close, we invited three or four of the Greek monks to lunch with us on the following Sunday. The provision of suitable viands was a somewhat difficult task, as, besides being professed vegetarians, they were then keeping the fast of the lesser Lent. Jacobos coquetted for some time, with the temptation of Julienne soup, but at last, yielding to the persuasive odour of the "Liebig" and the encouraging nudge of his companion, he consented to fall to. Their objection to flesh was fully counterbalanced by their fondness for preserves and their unlimited capacity for cognac.

CHAPTER VIII.

FROM SINAI TO SERBÁL.

Striking camp. Er Ráhah and the Nagb Hawa. Supperless halt. Wady Soláf; destructive flood. A Bedawí Poet. Feirán. We dismiss our Arabs; amusing scenes in consequence. Sheikh Hassan. Rephidim; the rock in Horeb; battle with the Amalekites; route from Rephidim to Sinai; Jebel Tahúnah. Hermits' cells.

THE special survey of Jebel Músa was now so far advanced that nothing more remained to be done but the delineation of the hill-features by the "hill-sketchers" of the Royal Engineers, whom we had brought with us. But, as this, involving tedious work on the bleak mountain tops, was impossible while the severely cold weather lasted, we decided to remove to Wády Feirán and begin operations in the neighbourhood of Jebel Serbál: accordingly by ten o'clock on New Year's day the once neat and symmetrical arc of tents, with the clean swept space in front, was one mass of bales, boxes and confusion. We had determined to go through the Nagb Hawa, taking with us the camels which carried the tents, but both 'Eíd, our former sheikh, and Embarek, whom he had brought with him as adjutant, declared that the road was impracticable; the discussion of this point caused a great deal of additional noise and squabbling. At last we allowed them to take the longer road round by Wády es Sheikh, on their promising to meet us in Wády Gharbeh at the other side of the pass; and after a frugal lunch of bread and figs, we started off for the appointed spot.

The morning was fine and clear, though rather hot; at breakfast the thermometer had stood at 22°, and we were now marching in a temperature of 95°. As we walked along the plain of Er Ráhah the effect of light upon the mountains was inexpressibly beautiful. On our left, whence the sun was shining, the rocks were tinted with various shades of the softest blue; while on our right, where the sunbeams fell directly upon the mountains, they shone out with a yellowish grey light, their outlines being so clearly defined that they looked like *silhouettes* against the liquid mirror of the sky. In the middle of the plain we came upon a small boulder, with "cup markings" such as Scotch antiquaries are familiar with, and of which the following account was given us by the Arabs. "The Auládd Jindí being deposed from their office as Ghafirs or protectors of the Convent, and the right of conducting pilgrims ceded to the Jibalíyeh, the chief men of the former tribe came to this stone, and in their anger declared that no Jebalí should ever pass that limit again, in confirmation of which oath they thrust their spears into the stone." There are slight objections to this story; the Arabs of Sinai do not carry spears, and the stone has evidently been removed, marks and all, to its present position. It is, however, a fact that the Bedawin do mark their borders with stones, and often inscribe rude symbols of their tribe upon them. We found several other stones with similar marks in various parts of the Peninsula, two in the Nagb Hawa, and the one in Wády ed Deir to which I have already alluded.

At the entrance of the Nagb Hawa is a thick bed of rushes and a tiny trickling stream; after this we come to a slight rise in the ground, from which the last glimpse of Sinai is obtained. The soil here is of a dark green colour, and is called *Kohli*, being supposed to contain a quantity of *Kohl* or antimony. Several huge scattered boulders of fantastic form are lying about; one of them, like the "Speaking Stone" before mentioned, has the appearance of being cleft in twain, and is called Madhrab Saif 'Edái, "My enemy's sword-stroke." The view beyond the pass from the crest of Er Ráhah is extremely beautiful. The plain seems enclosed by lofty mountain walls, and the gorge itself looks like a narrow gate, through which the open country and distant hills appear in the perfection of aerial perspective. As we saw it, with all the magical effect of sunset on the scene, these hills were glowing with a purple light against the ruddy sky; the foreground was of green and red, with golden light on every mountain peak, and streaks of crimson shot across the whole. Presently the background changed to a deep blue, which in turn gave way to a dark neutral tint; myriad stars shone out with silvery radiance, and night began.

By the time we had reached the other side of the pass it was quite dark, and, as we were getting both hungry and tired, we hailed with delight the appearance of a large bright flame in Wády Gharbeh, below the spot which had been appointed for our rendezvous and camping ground. But, on making for this, we found neither tents nor camels, only Wilson and Wyatt sitting over a log fire (for there was a *tarfah* grove here), and, near by, our four R. E. surveyors, with their Arab attendant Jumá. Now, after a long walk, undertaken on the strength of a few figs and a piece of bread, and after the fatigue of striking camp and anathematizing Bedawín from 7 A.M., the inward man requires refreshment and repose. A sandy bank and a pipe of "Cavendish" are insufficient of themselves to supply this want: need it therefore be wondered at that my remarks upon the conduct of the camel-drivers bore sarcastic reference to their grandfather's graves, and that I spoke the sentiments of the Expedition therein? There was nothing for it, however, but to wait patiently, and we passed the time in watching the fires which our Arabs kindled all around, and which produced a weird and picturesque effect. At last Jumá jumped up and screamed *Il ba'aráu jáiu*, "The camels are coming," and grateful visions of potted meat rose up before our eyes. But it was a false alarm; no one appeared but a solitary cameldriver, who had lingered behind at the starting, and now turned up at the tryst as puzzled and supperless as ourselves.

At last Sálem, who had gone on an exploring expedition of his own, appeared with two *fánúses* (paper lanterns), having discovered the camp at some distance. He reported that the camel-drivers had halted in a cold windy spot, without water or fuel, and were all sitting listlessly over their fires, not having even pitched the tents. We followed the old fellow in the dark through a labyrinth of rocky paths, and ultimately found the camp just as he had described it. Hastily putting up one tent, we had such dinner as could be provided under the circumstances, and, having liberally a-bused our sheikhs, sank into a peaceful sleep.

In the morning we found an agreeable change in the temperature, which was here much warmer, as we had descended about fifteen hundred feet on the previous day. Before reaching the spot where we had kindled our fires the evening before, we passed through a beautiful gorge filled with palms and tamarisks, a clear bright stream running in its bed; there were also garden walls, and many other signs of former cultivation. About four hours farther on, we came to a sharp turn in the wády, which here narrows into a defile, and, as soon as we had passed through this, found ourselves in a broad expanse, the entrance to Wády Soláf. We had kept the peak of Serbál in sight for the greater part of the day, but now the whole mountain rose up in all its azure grandeur before us.

This Wády Soláf was the scene of the great *seil*, or flood, in 1867, when an Arab encampment was washed away, and forty souls, together with many camels, sheep, and other cattle, perished in the waters. Mr. Holland was in Sinai at the time of the calamity, and narrowly escaped losing his life on the occasion. He describes the scene as something terrible to witness; a boiling, roaring torrent filled the entire valley, carrying down huge boulders of rock as though they had been so many pebbles, while whole families swept by, hurried on to destruction by the resistless course of the flood. The marks of devastation which it caused are still too plainly apparent, and I have seen the trunks of large palm-trees lying in the wády-bed at a distance of more than thirty miles from the place where they had grown. A single thunder-storm, with a heavy shower of rain, falling on the naked granite mountains, will be sufficient to produce these dreadful effects, and to convert a dry and level valley into a roaring river in a few short hours, thus realising the awful picture which David has drawn in the eighteenth Psalm:—" The Lord also thundered in the heavens, and the Highest gave his voice; hailstones and coals of fire. Then the channels of the waters were seen, and the foundations of the world were discovered at thy rebuke, O Lord." (Psalm xviii, 13, 15.)

The following is the translation of a poem composed on the occasion by Salámeh Abu Ta'imeh, one of our own camel-drivers, who had himself lost several friends and relatives in the flood. The language of the original is simple and unaffected, and the rhythm correct; as the *bonâ-fide* composition of an untutored son of the desert it may be not uninteresting to the English reader:—

> I dreamed a dream which filled my soul with fear,
>   Fresh grief came on me, but the wise have said,
> When sorrow cometh, joy is hovering near.
>   Methought I looked along a forest glade,
> And marvelled greatly how the trees did rear
>   Their heads to heaven; when lo! a whirlwind laid
> Their trunks all prostrate. Then I looked again,
>   And what but now like fallen trees had seemed
> Were forms of warriors untimely slain.
>   Again my fancy mocked me, and I dreamed
> Of storms and floods, of fierce resistless rain,
>   Of vivid lightnings that above me gleamed;—
> And yet again, dead men around me lay,
>   Dead men in myriads around me slept,
> Like the Great Gathering of the Judgment Day.
>   I woke—a torrent through the wády leapt,
> Nile had his ancient barriers burst away
>   And over Feirán's peaceful desert swept;
> Nor spared he any in his angry mood
>   Save one—to be the river-monsters' food!

Between five and six o'clock we reached our camp, which had been pitched in a shady spot, with colocynth gourds growing all around, the very *beau-idéal* of an Arabian scene. The next morning we followed the flat sandy watercourse of Wády Soláf. The year before, it had been a flourishing grove of tamarisk trees, but now nothing remained to show what it was but a few scattered roots half covered with boulders, which had lodged there in their passage down the valley. After a walk of seven miles, we reached El Buweib, the "gate," a narrow passage between the rocks about one hundred feet long by twenty wide, passing through which, we came presently to the palm-grove of Wády Feirán. This was one of the most delightful walks we had had since our sojourn in Sinai; the tall graceful trees afforded a delicious shade, fresh water ran at our feet, and, above all, *bulbuls* flitted from branch to branch uttering their sweet notes. It seemed to me a realisation of those dreams which the poetry of my favourite Persian poet, Háfiz, had so often inspired. Our camp was pitched, at length, in a lovely spot

Wády Feirán.

at the mouth of Wády 'Aleyát, a large open space completely surrounded by steep shelving mountains of gneiss, the fantastic cleavage and variegated colours of which added greatly to the beauty of the scene. Palms and tamarisks were dotted all around, and on every knoll and mountain slope were ruined houses, churches, and walls, the relics of the ancient monastic city of Paran. Behind our tents rose the majestic mass of Serbál, and beneath the rocky wall opposite ran a purling brook, only a few inches in depth, but still sufficiently cool, clear, and refreshing. When the heat of the day had gone by, we dined out in the open air, accompanied by the strains of a native minstrel, who played upon a *rebábeh*, and treated us to a romance of Abu Zeid, the great hero of Arabian song.

While we were at dinner, 'Eid, who had been in disgrace since the affair at Wády Gharbeh, came up, and, in spite of our struggles, insisted on kissing our hands all round. On our arrival at Feirán there had been a great disturbance with the Bedawín. The journey from the Convent is generally performed in two days, and, as they had caused us so much inconvenience by delaying us until the third, we determined to deduct something from their pay. This of course gave rise to many high words and violent gestures, which to one unacquainted with Arab manners would have seemed very terrible indeed. 'Eid himself at first protested loudly and vehemently, but when he found that we were inexorable, he lay down at my feet, literally grovelled in the dust, and, plucking his beard out by handfuls, besought me to beat him. At dinner he piteously repeated the request, and, on being told by Holland that "we were too busy then, but would beat him with pleasure when we had finished our meal," he exclaimed, *taiyeb*, "good", in a tone of intense satisfaction, and went off to take his money from the cook, to whom, as he had refused to accept the sum, we had consigned it. In the course of the evening we heard a great noise outside the tent; rushing out to see what was the matter, we found a large wolf fighting with some dogs which had strayed in from a neighbouring Arab encampment. It immediately made off, and, although we all turned out, armed with guns, revolvers and any thing that came to hand, and joined the dogs in the hunt, the beast managed to escape in the darkness of the night. All this would have been amusing enough, but we were anxious to finish our letters, and did not relish the interruptions.

The despatching of our post-bag on the following morning occasioned a fresh difficulty, for 'Eid and Embárek, whom we had felt compelled to discharge, had been exercising terrorism over the messenger we had selected, and declared that he should not set out for Suez. However, by threatening them with direst vengeance at the hands of the Consul,—the representative, in an Arab's eyes, of supreme earthly power,—we at last started him off. But it seemed as though we were not to have any peace; scarcely had he gone than I noticed the knot of Bedawín again in a state of great commotion, bandying something to and fro amongst them. This on inspection proved to be our own Arab guide, old Sálem, who, with his face bleeding, broke away from his tormentors, and informed me that he had been accused of stealing a purse containing a thousand piastres. The origin of this absurd charge was that Mr. Holland, amongst the *débris* of the flood in the previous year, had found an empty bag, and had taken it away as a curiosity. For want of some better object on which to vent their ill-temper, they had magnified this bag into a purse of money, and accused Sálem of stealing it. We had borne a great deal, but here was the last feather of the proverb, so, bringing out the choicest stores from my vocabulary, I rushed in among the sons of the desert, punched each turbaned head as it presented itself, and, following them to the outer limits of the camp, administered a hearty kick upon the hindermost, and saw their faces no more.

Having dismissed our Arabs, it was of course necessary to provide ourselves with another sheikh. We had not long to wait; for, hearing the state of the case, Hassan, the chief sheikh of the Towarah, lost no time in paying us a visit. He was a well-to-do Bedawí, with an easy but respectful mode of address, and a quiet demeanour that prepossessed us in his favour. We did not come to terms until much coffee had been consumed and the greater part of three days wasted in frequent discussions; but at last all was arranged, the contract written and sealed, and Hassan constituted our sole sheikh, *vice* 'Eid and Embárek deposed. Here a circumstance occurred which brought out his Bedawí cunning in an amusing way. Just as he was taking his departure, a son of old Mansúr's came up to the tent with an offer of service from his father, but we told him that we had just engaged some one else, and the young man retired. Hassan immediately bustled up, and asked what our visitor had said, and, on being told that it was no business of his, promptly demanded a copy of the document which we had just signed. This we gave him, and he went off in great satisfaction at our honesty and his own acuteness.

As he sat in our tent, many of the Arabs of the neighbourhood came up to salute him. I was much struck with their mode of addressing him; there was no obsequiousness, no sense of inferiority, and yet they treated his orders with a deference that was infinitely more respectful than any cringing recognition of his superior rank. For instance, we had expressed a wish for a *bedan*, and Hassan, turning to a hunter who was standing by, told him to go and look out for one. *Hádhir*, "ready," said the man, and throwing off his cloak and tarbúsh, a sure indication that he intended to hunt in earnest, he shouldered his gun and set off for the mountains. In the evening he returned with a fine ibex, which, in the then unsatisfactory state of our larder, was a most welcome arrival.

At Feirán we engaged as guide one of the natives of the place, who, being an experienced *bedan* hunter, was better acquainted than his fellows with the topography and nomenclature of the district around Serbál. He was one of the ugliest Bedawín I have ever seen, but a very cheerful willing fellow, never shrinking from the most fatiguing climb or grumbling at the heaviest load. He rejoiced in the name of Hisán el Harbí, and came of the 'Awárimeh, a respectable clan of the Towarah; he was extremely proud of his descent, and, though clad literally in rags and tatters, strutted about with an amusing assumption of aristocratic dignity.

We inaugurated our stay at Feirán by a great mutual hair-cutting; when it came to my turn to operate, I assumed the scissors with some diffidence, but, encouraged by the simple confidence with which my companion resigned himself into my hands, I set to work boldly upon his head. When I had finished, it presented precisely the appearance of a moth-eaten fur-reticule.

At the base of Serbál, in Wády Feirán, is a large and comparatively fertile tract, with a palm-grove which extends, notwithstanding the late destructive flood, for miles along the valley. It is, in fact, the most fertile part of the Peninsula, and one which the Amalekites would be naturally anxious to defend against an invading force; in this respect therefore it answers to the position of Rephidim. We should not expect a mere desert tribe, such as Amalek was, to sally forth in well-organized troops to meet the advancing hosts of Israel while the latter were yet in the comparatively open wilderness. Their immediate impulse, on the first intimation of the enemy's approach, would be to collect around their wells and palm-groves, and concert measures for protecting these their most precious possessions. When the hostile body had encamped within a short distance of the oasis, they would no doubt watch for an opportunity of attacking them unawares, in order to take them at a disadvantage before they could establish their camp or recover from their fatigues. Such would be the tactics of the modern Bedawín, and such, it appears from the Bible account, was the nature of the opposition which Israel encountered at Rephidim. They had "pitched in Rephidim", but the wells were defended, and they were obliged to halt on the outskirts of the fertile district, "and there was no water for the people to drink". Disappointed and fatigued, they "murmured against Moses, and said, Wherefore is this that thou hast brought us up out of Egypt, to kill us and our children and our cattle with thirst?" The miracle of striking the rock released them from this difficulty, and, as we are told immediately afterwards "then came Amalek, and fought with Israel in Rephidim." (Ex. xvii. 8.) But it is a significant fact that in Wády Feirán, immediately before the part of the valley where the fertility commences, I discovered a rock which Arab tradition regards as the site of the miracle. This rock, which has never before been noticed by travellers, is called Hesy el Khattátín, and is surrounded by small heaps of pebbles, placed upon every available stone in the immediate

neighbourhood; these are accounted for as follows:—
When the Children of Israel sat down by the miraculous stream and rested after their thirst was quenched, they amused themselves by throwing pebbles upon the surrounding pieces of rock. This has passed into a custom, which the Arabs of the present day keep up in memory of the event. It is supposed especially to propitiate Moses, and any one having a sick friend throws a pebble in his name, with the assurance of speedy relief.

The great objection to the identification of Feirán with Rephidim is that the Bible describes the next stage of the journey of the Israelites thus:—" For they were departed from Rephidim, and were come to the Desert of Sinai, and had pitched in the wilderness. And there Israel camped before the mount." (Exodus xix. 2.)

Now, if Jebel Músa be Sinai, it could hardly be reached in a single day's journey by any large host with heavy baggage. From Feirán the road is broad and open enough as far as the Nagb Hawa, but the laden camels must make a detour of some six or eight hours by the valley which comes in a little lower down to the left, namely Wády es Sheikh. The difficulty may be explained away on several hypotheses. First, the journey from Feirán to the Nagb Hawa may be considered as the last stage of the march, and when they had come to that pass, which forms, as it were, the gate of the Sinai district, they may be fairly said to have reached "the Desert of Sinai." The words, "and there Israel camped before the mount," seem to me to imply a separate operation, and I should be inclined to interpret the passage thus :—They were departed from Rephidim, or Feirán, and had reached the wilderness of Sinai, that is, the Sinai district at the mouth of the Nagb Hawa; and here they began to look out for a suitable place for a permanent camp. The spot chosen was the plain of Er Ráhah, "and there Israel camped before the mount." The operation of pitching the camp for so protracted a stay as they were about to make would occupy a longer period than usual, and may even have extended over several days, and yet be in strict accordance with the words of the Bible.

Again, it is quite possible that Moses and the chiefs of the elders took the short road through the pass, leaving the rest of the caravan with the heavy baggage to follow them round Wády es Sheikh and come into camp next morning. Captain Wilson and myself, being desirous on one occasion of pushing on to Jebel Músa by a certain day, actually adopted this expedient.

If it be objected that the distance from Feirán to the Pass is too long for a single day's journey, I would answer that a day's journey is not necessarily restricted to eight or nine hours, and that the Israelites probably travelled lightly equipped, as do the Arabs of the present day. These, when they wish to reach a particular spot in a given time, often travel for six or eight hours, and then, after a short rest, resume their journey and perform the remainder by night. The Arabic language has a word used specially to express this mode of travelling.

On reaching Wády Feirán, the traveller should first of all make a pilgrimage to the hill which I have just mentioned, as the probable station of Moses at the battle of Rephidim, not only because of the interest which, if the supposition be correct, attaches to the spot, but also because from this point he will obtain a clearer notion of the lie of the country than from any other.

VIEW FROM JEBEL TÁHÚNEH.

The hill, which is called Jebel Táhúneh (the Mountain of the Windmill), is not more than seven hundred feet high, and is situated on the northern side of the valley, immediately behind the mound on which the walls of the ancient convent stand.

Several chapels are found at short intervals along the path by which the ascent is made, and on the summit is the "oratorium," of which I have spoken, a small church with some ruined outbuildings attached to it. The original edifice was of dressed sandstone, but over the ruins of this are the remains of another and later building, constructed of rude stones taken from the mountain itself, and having the apse towards Jebel Serbál.

At the foot meanders Wády Feirán, with its grove of palms and tamarisks, while down from either flank of Mount Serbál, which faces you, run two steep wádies, 'Aleyát and 'Ajéleh. A huge basin of red rock, gneiss and porphyry, lies to the north, with the tall peak of Jebel el Benát standing out against the sky, and far away to the south-east, through an opening in the hills, is seen the long blue range of the Jebel Músa mountains. Clusters of ruined houses (remains of the ancient city of Paran) are dotted over the surrounding hills, and the rocky sides of the valley are perforated with innumerable tombs and hermits' cells.

I know of no ruins upon which one can gaze with so much satisfaction as on those of convents and hermitages; we do not, at least I do not, experience the same sadness which half mars the pleasure of contemplating a picturesque ruined town; the sadness of sympathy for a perished race of fellow-workers—the sadness of regret for useful works destroyed. Here one feels that only a just and fit consummation has been attained. The hermit has renounced his portion on earth, has sneered at nature's bounteous gifts, and in these ruins Nature is revenged. Looking only at the fancied merit of avoiding and shunning the temptations of the world, the recluse forgets that he is at the same time shirking the duties of that state of life to which it has pleased God to call him; and in seeking salvation by a life of penance, he is rather, like the Hindoo devotee, putting forth a claim against Heaven than endeavouring to deserve God's favour by a cheerful submission to His will. To shun temptation by putting oneself out of its reach argues both want of confidence in one's power to resist evil, and of distrust in God's help.

CHAPTER IX.

FEIRÁN.

Burial ground of Sheikh Abu Shebíb. Date-palms and gardens. El Maharrad; ruins of the ancient convent. Monkish tombs. Jebel Serbál. Wády 'Aleyát; treasure-finders again; a storm; Jebel Moneijáh; death in the Arab camp. Wády 'Ajeleh. Ascent of Serbál; the summit; beacon-fires; meaning of the name Serbál. Abu l' Hosein, the fox; Visit to Sheikh Hassan; a heavy dinner; an Arabian night's entertainment.

NEAR our camp, in the midst of the palm-grove, was a diminutive Arab village, consisting of a few wooden huts, the residents in which make a scanty livelihood by growing tobacco and selling it to the Bedawín who pass that way. Our own Arabs used the place as an hostelry when waiting for orders about the camels, and on such occasions made night hideous by the monotonous and unseasonable music to which the sons of the desert are addicted.

Here too is a burial-ground with several nicely kept graves, one of them ornamented with a white marble headstone carved in a pretty lily pattern, a relic of the ruined convent church close by. This cemetery, as usual, contains a "Weli," the tomb of Sheikh Abu Shebíb, the patron saint of the district. It is a small stone building, rather neatly kept for a Bedawí institution, and the cenotaph in the centre is actually covered with a *kisweh*, or cotton pall. A powerful odour of sanctity pervades the place, and is believed to be particularly pernicious to false swearers, so that, if a person suspected of any crime consent to "swear by the tomb of Abu Shebíb," it is considered as a conclusive proof of his innocence. The Peninsula of Sinai is divided into so many districts, each of which has its own private saint. In every "parish" an acacia (or shittim) tree is consecrated, and is not mutilated by having its branches rudely lopped off to feed the flocks withal, the fate of every other tree of the species. The pods are shaken off when ripe, as they form a favourite and nutritious food for the camels; but even for this the saint's permission is first formally asked at his tomb. The Arab regards his patron with as profound a reverence as that with which an Italian peasant looks upon his little copper Januarius. He appeals to him for help on every occasion of difficulty, and a very edifying *acta sanctorum* might be compiled from the accounts given of their miraculous interference. Abu Shebíb himself is reported to have appeared in answer to the prayers of a hunter who had broken his leg on Jebel el Benát, and to have conveyed him safe and sound to his own home. True, however, even after death, to his Arab instincts, the saint stipulated for a handsome *bakh-*

shish, a white-faced sheep to be offered once every year at his tomb.

The dates of this palm-grove are some of the finest in Egyptian territory. Each tree has its owner, whose rights are respected without the necessity of setting fences or walls around to protect the fruit: indeed this would be impossible, as the property is in the tree itself, and not in the soil, and many of the richer Bedawín own a number of palms scattered singly or in groups throughout the plantation. The fruit when gathered is pressed tightly into bags of goats' skin, and moistened with a little oil or butter, in which state it retains its freshness and flavour for a considerable length of time. Besides the palms, there are many *sidr* trees, (bearing a small acrid fruit called *nebbuk*,) and occasional patches of corn or garden land. The irrigation is entirely performed by the *shádúf*, a long pole, with a bucket at the upper end and a heavy weight attached to the lower and shorter one, by which means the water is drawn from the well and poured into channels, or distributed over the land with the least possible labour.

Palms are always pretty and picturesque, but here their beauty is enhanced by the branches being left for the most part untrimmed, by the gorgeous diversity of colouring in the rocks on either side of the valley, and by the pleasant little stream that flows along its bed.

Emerging from the grove, we come upon the ruins of the ancient city, situated upon an elevation called El Maharrad, in the centre of the valley, between the mouths of wádies 'Aleyát and 'Ajeleh. They consist of the foundations of an old monastic establishment, of which nothing now remains above ground but part of the church walls and a few broken columns and entablatures. Amongst the latter we found a curiously carved stone, containing the figure of a man in a sitting posture with his arms raised aloft; it was probably intended as a representation of Moses at the Battle of Rephidim, and, if so, would confirm the supposition that this spot is the traditional site of the defeat of the Amalekites. At the north end of the Maharrad is the mouth of a cave or well, supposed to communicate with subterranean vaults beneath the ruins, and the Arabs declare that stores of wheat and treasures of untold wealth lie concealed in its mysterious depths.

We spent one or two very pleasant afternoons grubbing about in the ash-heap and crypt of this old monastery, and were rewarded for our labour by finding sundry pieces of monk, pottery, coins, and other interesting relics of antiquity.

Many of the stones from the church have been removed and employed by some later race in building rude dwelling houses. A little colony of these stands on the north side of the valley; but they have been deserted in their turn, and are now used only as storehouses by the Arabs. On some of them we found pieces of carving, and one or two imperfect Greek inscriptions. The sides of Wády Feirán are excavated with innumerable tombs and cells, and indeed the place must have been a perfect hermit-warren in its palmier days. The hill tops also are covered in every direction with small square *nawámis*, apparently monkish graves; the bodies lie east and west, and in one or two which we opened there were traces of a coarse shroud and wooden coffin. Above the body was a flat stone, forming a shelf in the upper part of the tomb; but this did not seem in any instance to have contained a second interment, and we were unable to discover the use for which it was intended. A little below Jebel Táhúnch there is a group of these erections, forming a series of catacombs or chambers which might at a distance be mistaken for a two-storied house.

When seen from a distance Serbál presents a boldness of outline and an appearance of massive isolation which entitled it to rank as one of the grandest and most distinctive features of the Peninsula. Although inferior in height to many of the other mountains it commands a more extensive prospect than even Katarína or Umm Shomer.

On the southern side it descends towards the plain of El Gá'ah in rugged and almost inaccessible slopes. From the extremities of its northern front two rough and stony valleys run down into Wády Feirán; that at the eastern end is called 'Aleyát and that at the western, 'Ajelch. The space between these is a tumbled and chaotic mass of mountains, rising at their highest point, Jebel Abu Shíah, to an elevation of 2500 feet above Feirán. There is no plain at its base and, indeed, absolutely no spot which would afford standing room for any large number of persons even within sight of the mountain. The author of " The tent and the Khán" considers Wády 'Aleyát "sufficiently ample to have contained the tents of all the children of Israel," while others who support the claims of Serbál to be the true Sinai would make the space between the two valleys the site of the encampment. Now

JEBEL SERBÁL.

it happens unfortunately for the first theory that Wády 'Aleyát is so thickly strewn with huge boulders and so worn and broken up by the torrents which have from time to time rushed through it, that it is difficult to pick your way along, and there are but few places in the whole valley where even a small number of tents could be pitched. With

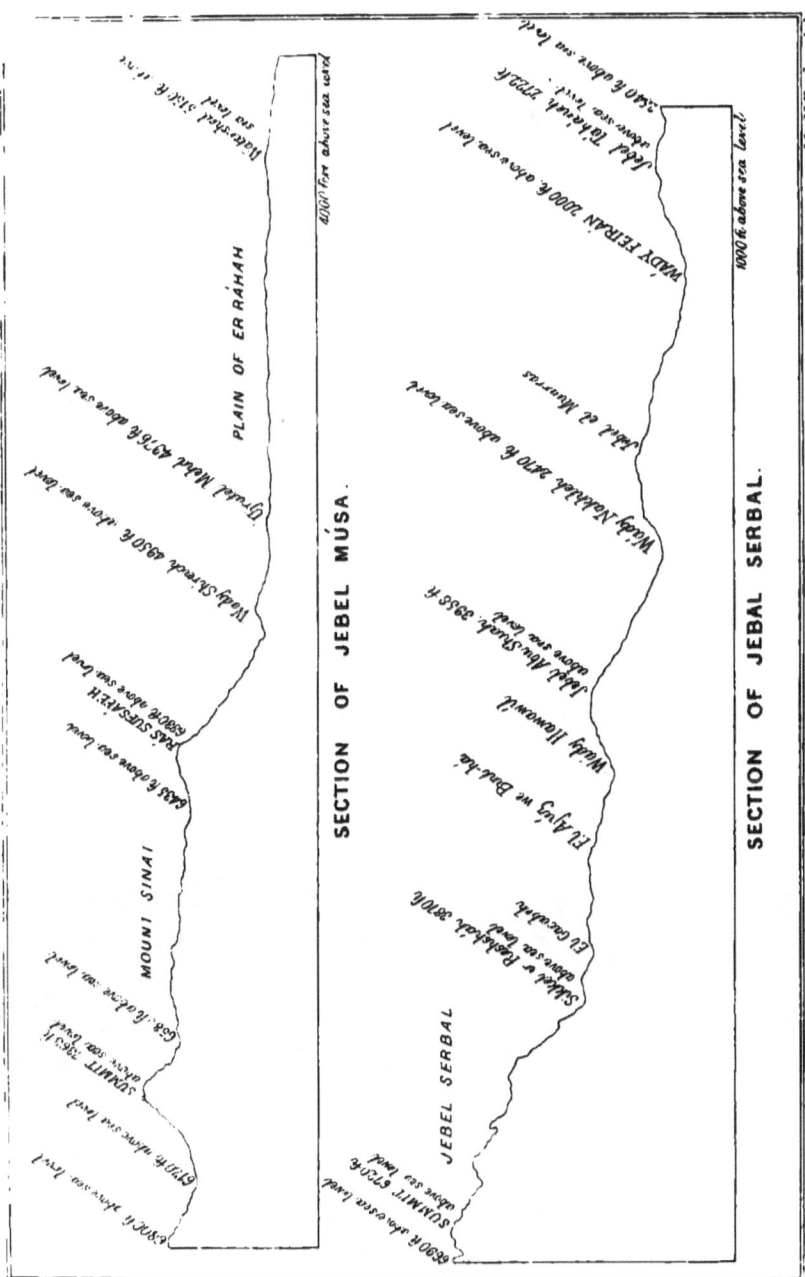

Reduced from the Sections of the Sinai Survey Expedition

regard to the second hypothesis, I have already shown that the two wádíes are separated by a rugged mountain mass and this would have been, to say the least, an exceedingly inconvenient camping ground for the children of Israel. The view from Jebel Táhúneh, on page 162, will illustrate my position far better than any description could do; and a comparison of the sections of Jebel Músa and Jebel Serbál must convince even the most sceptical how incomparably better the former mountain answers to the requirements of the Bible narrative. Views of Serbál may be obtained from various parts of Feirán, but they are mere glimpses, and there is no spot where a large number of spectators could assemble together and be said to stand "before the Mount."

A well-known writer on Sinai and its inscriptions, remarkable alike for the ingenuity and impossibility of his theories, has fancied that he detects in the name 'Ajeleh an allusion to the calf ('Ejl) which the Israelites worshipped, and adduces it as a strong argument in support of the identity of Serbál with Sinai. The real fact is that the word implies "haste" or "quickness," and, on enquiring of the Arabs why it was so called, the invariable answer was, "Because it is a quick road to Tor," which it undoubtedly is.

Wády 'Aleyát is filled with dark-green acacia trees, which, standing out in bold relief against the grey rocks, give it the appearance of some huge boulevard. At the upper end are two groves of palm-trees, the higher containing a charming little piece of landscape which well repays the traveller for a pilgrimage to the spot. A large white boulder rests upon the rocky bed of the valley, and from beneath it runs a tiny mountain stream; on the left are some graceful feathery palms, and on the right a wall of the most lovely pink porphyry, its colour relieved by the herbs and flowers that grow in the clefts and chinks. Near this spot the Arabs show a hole dug in the ground, in which they say that an immense treasure was discovered by one of the Maghrabí soothsayers of whom I have before spoken. The story has rather more of romance about it than most of these accounts. A Bedawí was walking one day in Cairo, when a man whom he had never seen before accosted him and invited him into his house. After hospitably entertaining him, the stranger, a Maghrabí of course, informed him that his magic arts had revealed the existence of an immense treasure in Wády 'Aleyát, and offered to share it with him if he would conduct him to the spot. They set out together, found the treasure as it had been described, and, having laden their camel with gold, were returning home, when the Bedawí conceived the idea of murdering his benefactor and appropriating all the spoil. But the magician was too subtle for him, and just as the Arab's finger was upon the trigger of his matchlock he suddenly threw a little dust behind him, and the traitor fell to the ground blinded. On his way back to Suez, however, the Maghrabí repented, and not only sent back a remedy which restored the other's sight, but is said to have taken the unnecessary trouble of writing over the Báb en Nasr (one of the old gates of Cairo) the words, "Cursed be he who blinds a Bedawí."

My first acquaintance with Wády 'Aleyát was made on the eve of a heavy storm; and grand indeed it was to hear the wind roaring amidst the crags of the gigantic mountain. I hurried home, telling my Arab guide to make haste, unless he wished to get wet through. He, poor fellow, had no notion of reading the sky for indications of the weather, and professed the greatest astonishment at my prophecy of the coming rain. When, in order to enlighten him still further, I carefully explained the use and construction of a barometer, he listened attentively, and observed, "I suppose you can stop the rain as well as bring it?"—a nice example of the advantage of popularising science.

About half way up Wády 'Aleyát, on the left hand, is a mountain named, like that at Jebel Músa, Moneiját, "the Mount of the Conference." The Arabs, while they attach no sanctity or importance whatever to Serbál, regard this little mountain with profound veneration, and sacrifice to Moses upon it once every year. On the summit is a small enclosure of rude stones, in which they are accustomed to leave some votive offerings whenever they visit the spot, and the ground is covered with beads, pieces of old camel rope, human hair, and other relics of the faithful. When I made the ascent, I borrowed a *zemzemíyeh,* or small waterskin, from an old woman in the neighbourhood, as I wished to take some paper squeezes of the Sinaitic inscriptions with which the walls of the enclosure are covered. At first the owner was unwilling to lend it, fearing, as she said, that "I might take it into my head to leave it on the top as an offering to the saint!" The sacrifices here are, as usual, followed by a *mesámereh,* or serenade, the whole assembly singing in chorus—

"Ya m'neiját Músa tálibín testúrak,
Teslim el ajáwíd kull senneh enzúrak."

"Oh, place of Moses' conference, we seek thy privilege! Save the good folk, and we will visit thee every year."

In Wády 'Aleyát was an Arab encampment, and during our stay in the neighbourhood a death occurred in one of the tents. The wailing of the women on the occasion was loud and passionate, and would have been touching had it not been too energetic. I saw the mother and sister of the departed sitting by the roadside howling horribly: the old lady especially distinguished herself, and appeared to me as an inpartial observer, to be continually watching for opportunities of boxing her own ears unawares, and when she had thus succeeded in arousing herself, she renewed her lamentations, shrieking out, "*Ya b'naiye wain elyák!*"—"Oh, my son, where shall I find thee!" Within a few hours of his decease, the defunct was decently interred in a *námús* in the vicinity.

On the right hand of Wády 'Aleyát is a valley

called Nakheleh, heading in the rugged mass of hills which stretches down from the foot of Serbál; though very steep and difficult of ascent, from the number of loose boulders brought down by the floods, it still bears traces of an ancient road passing over the watershed into Wády 'Ajeleh. The course of this road is marked by a line of Sinaitic inscriptions, and a side path on the left leads up to the summit of Abu Shíah, the highest point of the spur.

WÁDY 'AJELEH FROM THE WATERSHED.

Wády 'Ajeleh is much more steep and rugged than Wády 'Aleyát, the watershed being two thousand feet above the level of Wády Feirán. It contains nothing of interest but the ruins of a small building, probably a fort, on one of the mountains at the western side of the valley. The summit of this mountain consists of one huge round block of white granite, from which it receives the name of Sullá'. It is probably identical with the Jebel Latrum, mentioned by Dr. Robinson, to which the monks were wont to retreat when harassed by the Saracens, its height and position admirably adapting it for such a purpose. In addition to the walls and other buildings, large stones are artfully arranged along the edge of the precipice, ready to be rolled down on the head of any one who might venture to approach the sanctuary with hostile intent.

As I was hunting about for inscriptions in this neighbourhood, I espied a rock covered with some unusual characters, which, however, on nearer inspection, proved to be merely natural markings on the stone. "Ah," said old Salem, who had accompanied me, and noticed the mistake, "that's God's writing, not a Bedawí's." The simple piety of the remark impressed me greatly. The religious instincts of these people are very strongly developed, and the frequent *inshallah, kháf allah,* and the like, with which they interlard their discourse, seem to proceed from a really conscious feeling of the omnipresence of Deity, and not to be, as with many Arabs, mere expletives or forms of speech.

The day had been a cloudy one, and as I returned to camp the last dull pink shades of sunset were dying away, when suddenly the whole scene was lit up as if by magic, and the light fleecy clouds that were flitting across the sky were turned in a moment into masses of golden light: a more beautiful effect of the after-glow I have never seen in the East either before or since.

An amusing incident occurred the next morning as we sat at breakfast. 'Eisa, our Syrian man-servant, rushed into the tent, closely followed by a frying-pan, and exclaimed in voluble Arabic, and with frantic gestures, that the cook had insulted him and beaten him. "And now," said he, pointing to the missile which had come unpleasantly near our heads, "now he's throwing the kitchen at me!"

The ascent of Serbál was an event to which we had all looked forward with pleasurable anticipation. To avoid the long and troublesome walk to the base of the mountain, we determined to encamp the night before in Wády 'Aleyát, and make an early start in the morning. Accordingly, on the 13th of January, our new sheikh Hassan appeared with three camels, to carry our beds and stores to the place which we had selected. At first, the loading proceeded quietly enough; but presently a deputation of the Arabs headed by the Sheikh himself arrived to say that they could not carry the things unless they were allowed to take another camel.

"You can't go, then, without a fourth camel?" I asked.

"Quite impossible," replied Sheikh Hassan gleefully, with a look of intelligence at the others, as much as to say that the Khawáját were taking the matter a great deal more quietly than he had expected.

"Very well," said I: "have the goodness to take

off those loads, and never let me see your faces again."

In five minutes everything was packed upon the three beasts, and we were ready to start. We had taken no tents, but made our beds in the open air, sleeping none the less soundly for occasional showers of rain which fell during the night. At about half-past seven we commenced the ascent. An earlier hour had been fixed; but the morning broke so cloudy and unpromising, that we were obliged to wait until a clearing sky encouraged us to proceed. Selecting the western side of the mountain, we went up by a previously unexplored path, and in about an hour and a half reached the base of the great domes of rocks which compose the summit. Here some time was consumed in dividing the working parties and selecting the most favourable points for observation. Half an hour more brought us to the actual summit, the ascent having been made without any other halt than that just mentioned; but, from our experience at Jebel Músa, we were all in capital training, and did not find the climb so toilsome and difficult as it has been described.

The topmost peak of Serbál consists of a series of rounded crags, separated by deep and rugged ravines, and commanding a fine view of the country around, though less comprehensive and characteristic than that from Jebel Katarína. The highest point is called El Madhawwa (the Lighthouse), and is covered, as well as the roads leading up to it, with

Sinaitic inscriptions: some of these have been executed in white paint, or whitewash, and owing to their sheltered position on the walls of a cavern have perfectly withstood the ravages of time. On the lower of the two bluffs of which the summit consists is a ring of stones, the remains of the erection on which beacon-fires were lighted at the approach of invaders, or other danger, when Sinai was better populated than it is now. Other similar beacon-towers are found in various mountain heights throughout the Peninsula, and a regular system of such signals seems to have existed along the road from Syria to Egypt. That under consideration has been described as "a Druidical circle," which reminds me of other misconceptions to which the theories concerning Serbál have given rise.

In their desire to discover traces of traditional importance attaching to the spot which they would identify with the Mountain of the Law, many writers have asserted that the name itself, Serbál, is but a corruption of Ser Ba'al, Lord Baal, and declare that it was consecrated, in pagan times, to the worship of that divinity. Now, the word Ba'al contains the very impracticable Semitic consonant 'ain, which—however insignificant it may sound to European ears—could never drop out or be confounded with the simple á of the word Serbál. Others again have sought to identify it with the name of the Indian God Shiva! The word, in fact, signifies "a shirt," and is often metaphorically employed by Arabic writers to describe a large body of water pouring over such smooth rounded surfaces as those of which the summit is composed, and is exactly analogous in this respect to our own expression, "a sheet of water." Thus does the very philology to which it appeals prove fatal to this attractive and plausible theory. Men are too apt, alas!, to confound the overthrow of their own theories with a denial of the facts themselves which they have taken so much trouble to assert. But, if they were content to apply to questions of sacred topography the same impartial criticism by which they would judge of scientific facts, the cause of truth would prosper better than by such attempts to establish it on weak or insufficient grounds.

A grand but disappointing effect in the landscape was produced by a large bank of clouds, lit up by the morning sun, which bore down directly upon us and threatened to put a sudden stop to the work of observation; but luckily they dispersed sufficiently to permit of angles being taken to the most important points, although the top of Serbál itself, the plain of El Gá'ah, and the range of mountains from Jebel Músa to Umm Shomer, were from time to time enveloped in mist and quite shut out of sight.

When the observing was concluded, all hands were employed in the laborious and somewhat perilous task of carrying stones up the steep slippery rocks, for the purpose of building cairns upon the summit, and, this having been satisfactorily accomplished, we descended by the eastern end of the mountain. The last was by no means the least fatiguing part of the day's work, for the only path is by a slide, which resembles a newly macadamised Brobdignagian road tilted on end, and it is no easy thing to jolt for two hours over boulders, each as large as a Pickford's van.

An incident occurred during the day which exhibits in a very favourable light the docile character of the Towarah Bedawín. We had selected five men to carry up the instruments, but on arriving at the base of the highest peak we found that a sixth had shouldered one of the boxes, and joined the party for the purpose of sharing in the spoils. As we had not hired him, we told him to go back, and assured him that he would get nothing for coming so far; not that the statement was strictly true, but principle had to be maintained at any cost to other people's feelings. "Am I really to go?" he pleaded piteously. "In peace," we replied, and down he accordingly trotted. On returning to camp in the evening this man was among the first to welcome us, and by his cheerful, willing demeanour did all he could to show that he was not aggrieved. In acknowledgment of his good behaviour we subsequently gave him a bakhshish twice as large as he would otherwise have received.

A few days afterwards, Mr Holland and I, in accordance with a promise made to Sheikh Hassan, prepared to pay a visit to the tents of the Auláïd Sa'íd. The morning on which we were to have started was a thoroughly wet one, and we were of course obliged to put off our journey and stay in camp for that day.

Taking advantage of a lull in the showers, Holland let out a little fox which an Arab had caught for him, and which is now in the Zoological Gardens in Regent's Park; one of the camel-drivers who was standing near watched the animal's gambols for some time with great admiration, and finally delivered himself of the following remark: "Ah! he is a clever little fellow this Abu 'l Hosein.* He catches the hares although they are quite as big as himself, and eats them. He manages to catch them by coming up to them in a friendly way and tickling them with his tail; then just as they are beginning to enjoy the fun, he fastens on their throat, and kills them."

The Arabs have, like most other nations, many quaint stories concerning the wonderful sagacity of the fox. One of these is worth recording: Two travellers had halted in the desert, and had just killed a couple of fowls for their dinner. Before they could dress the birds, the hour of prayer arrived, and they turned, like good Muslims, to their devotions. A fox which had been skulking in the neighbourhood, seeing them thus engaged, came boldly up and carried off one of the fowls before their very eyes. Prayers over, they began lamenting over their loss, when, to their amazement, they

* Abu 'l Hosein, "father of the little fortress," is the common Arab nick-name for a fox.

beheld the thief at a little distance dragging his tail submissively behind him, and holding the fowl in his mouth; he then deposited it on the ground, and slunk away with every sign of repentance and contrition. They at once hailed the occurrence as a miraculous testimony to their own piety, and ran to pick up the fowl which had been thus strangely restored to them: on reaching the spot, however, they found that Reynard had only restored the skin, and in the mean time had slyly stolen round to their camp-fire, and made off with the remaining moiety of their dinner.

At last we started, and accompanied by 'Ali and Selámeh, two of the Sheikh's relations whom he had sent with dromedaries to convey us, came to Wády el Akhdhar, where his people were encamped, and were received at the door of the tent by the sheikh himself with profuse and patriarchal expressions of welcome. Entering the *khatt es sherif*, or chief apartment, we found that it had been carefully swept and prepared for our reception, and two thin but pretty carpets spread along the wall of the harem, whence the voices of women and children proceeded in tones which argued badly for our night's repose. Taking off our boots, we sat down upon the carpets, and went through the ceremony of patting our breasts and exchanging salutations with every individual present, as Arab etiquette demands. Next came the no less important ceremony of drinking coffee, which was prepared by Sálem, our polite but discarded Serbál attendant, assisted by a poor member of the Jibalíyeh tribe, who had attached himself to the camp for the nonce, and was earning a scanty livelihood by doing odd jobs for the Arabs, receiving in turn a modicum of their leavings. He had a little daughter and a bad toothache, and was silent and morose throughout the evening.

The Arab process of coffee-making is as follows:—The berries are first roasted, and then transferred into an earthenware pipkin, and ground by turning a large stick rapidly round in it. The contents, when pounded, are poured into the *bakraj*, or coffee-pot, in which water with sugar in it has been previously set to boil, any particles that may still cling to the sides of the pipkin being carefully swept together with a brush of palm fibre attached to it for the purpose. The host, or his deputy, then removes the pot from the fire, and having washed out the *finjáns*, or tiny coffee-cups, drinks first himself, in accordance with a time-honoured Eastern custom, and then presents it to his guests. Our coffee over, we lit the solemn *chibouk* and awaited dinner. It was served shortly after sunset, and the apprehensions with which I had been regarding it were nowise diminished by the appearance of the viands themselves. They consisted of three wooden bowls of plain boiled meat, and two other bowls of bread, that is to say of unleavened cake, mashed up with onions and the liquor in which the meat had been boiled. Bowls of meat containing the more delicate morsels were set before Holland and myself, and we were also provided with one huge bowl of bread between us. The sheikhs then proceeded to hand round the rest of the meat to their assembled retainers and friends, and waited patiently for us to invite them to partake of our portions. This, after some pressing, they consented to do, and Hassan and I, Holland and 'Ali, were soon engaged in picking out *bonne-bouches* with our fingers, and thrusting them into each other's mouths. A great treat, for the season of the year, was also provided for us in the shape of a draught of milk, which although slightly flavoured with '*abeitherán*, the nastiest of all "the desert's spicy stores," was not unacceptable.

Having swallowed much more than was good for me, and after some difficulty convinced the unbelieving sheikh of my physical incapacity to hold any more, the meal came to an end, and water was brought us to wash our hands, an attention which had also been paid us before dinner. The washing was second-hand, our friend sprinkling it over us with his own fingers as an additional mark of politeness. Coffee and pipes were then brought in—a very necessary sedative after so much alimentary exertion—and for some time we engaged in quiet and digestive conversation.

Presently 'Ali took up a *rebábeh* or native lute, and, after tuning up to his satisfaction, commenced singing some excruciating songs, occasionally varying the performance by improvising a verse or two in our honour, for they are a poetical family, these sheikhs of the Aulád Sa'íd. In the course of the evening it was intimated that, if we pleased, a *mesámerah* should be got up for our delectation; but, as many of the men were away at Cairo buying corn, we were told that we must not expect a grand *fantasia*. Of course we expressed the greatest delight, and Sálem, the ladies' man of the encampment, was despatched to collect the necessary females. Being invited to join in the entertainment, we accompanied the sheikh and party outside the tent, and standing in a row, with our hands clasped in a prayerful attitude, we commenced singing for the ladies to come. The words and intonation of our caterwaul may be thus represented:—

"Hai-ya koom Alláhu yá summâr't el láilá-á-h...*humphfh*."

"God bless you, ye nightly serenaders."

When we had repeated this for about a quarter of an hour, the women, all closely veiled, made their appearance, and after a great deal of unnecessary fuss arranged themselves in a group in the centre; whereupon we recommenced our song, this time in an amœbeic howl.

I now suggested that the dancing should begin, and our Semitic M.C. hurried the ladies on by shouting *Háti jemalain*, "Bring a couple of camels;" for under this choice metaphor the fair sex is always addressed on such occasions. Presently "the camel" appeared, and commenced what Burckhardt has described as "graceful and delicate motions," but which reminded me forcibly of a top-heavy hollyhock, the dancer remaining on one spot, and merely swaying herself to and fro in a ridiculous and awkward manner. All this time the men were encouraging her to fresh exertions, by the same cries by which they urge on their camels, such as *hait, hait! 'arr-rij!* and the like euphonious sounds.

Tired at last of our entertainment, we returned into the tent, and after some more coffee and pipes lay down to sleep. On awaking next morning we found our entertainers seated round the fire, and breakfast ready, and, as our toilette was an exceedingly simple one, we did not keep them waiting long. The meal was very like our dinner of the night before, and the mode of feeding the same. When I had just congratulated myself on having finished, the graceless Hassan discovered the sheep's heart, and insisted upon my eating it. I accordingly prepared to sacrifice digestion to etiquette, to the great delight of my fellow-traveller, but, as he was himself dextrously manipulating a large bone at the moment, I was enabled to reply with a *tu quoque* to his good-humoured "chaff."

It was a pretty sight to witness the return of the flocks to camp at night. As soon as the bells were heard tinkling in the distance, the little kids begin to skip about in the most insane manner, and, bleating frantically, single out and run up to their respective dams. In the morning the animals range themselves in front of the tent, and wait until the word of command is given, when they sally forth again to their mountain pasturage. I must, however, confess that I am not sufficiently Arabicised to appreciate the goat as a drawing-room companion; he has an unpleasant habit of making a wild attack upon you for the possession of your tobacco-pouch, and of accepting imaginary challenges to a butting-match, and thus upsetting you at inopportune moments.

At last our visit came to an end, and we were escorted back to camp by the sheikh himself, for Arab hospitality demands that a host shall accompany his guest a day's journey on the road. We returned by Wády Khabár, a pretty valley which flows into Wády Feirán; here we found numbers of Sinaitic inscriptions, the greater portion of them clustered, as usual, around a shady spring. The mouth of this wády affords a good instance of a geological feature peculiar, I believe, to the desert; large *jorfs*, or gravel-banks, cut through by the floods, and showing in section the former levels of the wády-bed.

CHAPTER X.

MUKATTEB AND MAGHÁRAH.

Journey down Wády Feirán. Wády Mukatteb. The Sinaitic Inscriptions; their nature and authorship. Visit from Sheikh Mansúr. Alone in the Wilderness. Wády Igné; Egyptian mines and hieroglyphic tablets. Anecdotes of the Arabs. An outlaw. Major Macdonald's house. An Egyptian military station. Instruments employed by the miners. "Sinai Photographed." The "Bat Cave."

On the 25th of January Mr Holland and I left Feirán, and started for Wády Mukatteb, "the Valley of the Inscriptions." Passing through the pretty palm-grove of El Hesweh, below our camp, we came to Hesy el Khattátín (of which I have before spoken as the traditional rock struck by Moses), continued our walk down Wády Feirán for about twelve miles, and encamped some time after night-fall beneath a rock called Jum'at el Beidh. There was little to remark on our journey down until we reached Jebel Mukatteb on the following afternoon. Here the wády widens out almost into a plain, and low blocks of limestone and sandstone take the place of the rugged igneous rocks to which we had been so long accustomed. A narrow pass on the right led us into Wády Mukatteb itself, which, though a magnificent piece of scenery, was quite different from the ideal picture I had formed of it from previous descriptions. It is a broad open valley, with low sloping hills on one side and a few fine mountains on the other. Beneath the low hills are several isolated plateaux, from which a mass of broken rock has here and there slipped down, and it is on the smooth faces of these stones that the inscriptions occur. Like those which we had met with on

WÁDY MUKATTEB.

the granite district, they are mere scratches on the rock, the work of idle loungers, consisting, for the most part, of mere names interspersed with rude figures of men and animals. In a philological point of view they do possess a certain interest, but otherwise the "Sinaitic inscriptions" are as worthless and unimportant as the Arab, Greek, and European *graffiti* with which they are interspersed. The language employed is Aramæan, the Semitic dialect which in the earlier centuries of our era held throughout the East the place now occupied by the modern Arabic, and the character differs little from the Nabathæan alphabet used in the inscriptions of Idumæa and central Syria. Thus far they accord with the account given of them by Cosmas Indicopleustes in the 6th century; I see no reason why, without for a moment admitting a too remote origin, we should not believe that his Jewish fellow-travellers read, as he asserts that they did, inscriptions in a language and character so cognate to their own. It is not true that they are found in inaccessible places high up on the rock, nor do we ever meet with them unless there is some pleasant shade or a convenient camping ground close by. In such places they exist in a confused jumble, reminding one forcibly of those spots which tourist Cockneyism has marked for its own. The instrument used appears to have been a sharp stone, by which they were dotted in; a single glance is sufficient to convince the inquirer that neither care nor uniformity has been aimed at in their execution. They have been attributed entirely to Christian pilgrims, but, although some of them are undoubtedly their work, the other localities in which they are found renders it extremely improbable that they can be assigned exclusively to this class. Wády Mukatteb, being on the main road through the country, has, as might be expected, a large, even the largest, share, but there are many other remote spots in Sinai where they are scarcely less numerous. In the more flourishing times of the peninsula, and especially during the monkish occupation, there must have been *sûks*, or public marts, and even permanent colonies of traders, to supply the wants of the inhabitants; and those who frequented the fairs, speaking and writing the then prevalent dialect of the East, would be as likely to leave *graffiti* behind them as do their successors in other parts of the desert in the present day. Thus we find Sinaitic as well as Greek inscriptions not only on all the principal roads, but wherever shade, water, or pasture would attract a concourse of men; and they occur as far as the camel-roads extend, especially in the vicinity of the ruined monasteries; but, where these are perched upon the inaccessible rocks or at the places of pilgrimage themselves, they are, with few exceptions, seldom found. Serbál, which served as a beacon tower, and consequently became a secular place of gathering, has many such inscriptions, but Sinai's hallowed chapels and confessional archways are without a trace of them. I imagine, then, that the greater part of the inscriptions are due to a commercial people, traders, carriers, and settlers in the land. No less than twelve of those which we copied were bilingual, being written in Greek and Sinaitic by one and the same hand. The existence of one of these was previously known: it differs from the rest in being carefully cut with a chisel and enclosed by a border line. That many of the writers were Christian is proved by the number of Christian signs which they used, but it is equally clear from internal evidence that a large proportion of them were Pagans. They must have extended far down into the later Monkish times, possibly until the spread of el Islám brought the ancestors of the present inhabitants, Bedawín hordes from Arabia proper, to the mountains of Sinai, and dispersed or absorbed that Saracen population of which the Monks stood in such mortal fear.

Soon after our arrival, we were honoured with a visit from our former sheikh, Mansúr, and his reception and entertainment occupied at least an hour and a half of our valuable time. As a specimen of desert etiquette, it may not be uninteresting to describe his arrival. A weather-beaten old sheikh, his head wrapped in a bright-coloured *kefíyeh*, and wearing a black '*abbah* and a sheepskin loosely thrown across his shoulders, rides up on a gaily caparisoned dromedary, accompanied by a younger person on a less pretending animal. "*Kh—kh—kh*" go the salival glands of both, as an intimation to the camels to kneel, and these intelligent animals at once set up a hideous moan, as though in direst anguish, and, twisting round their long necks, regard their riders with mingled indignation and contempt. At last, and quite unexpectedly, the beasts flop down upon their fore-legs, and after an interval follow suit with their hinder parts. But old Mansúr is a practised rider and slides off with an easy and dignified air. "*Ahlan wa sahlan ya Mansúr!*" "Welcome, Mansúr!" exclaim both Holland and myself, striking at the same time a sentimental attitude with our hands upon our breasts. "*Selamát*," "Peace," replies the old fellow, and we then proceed to inquire after his health, repeating the question half a dozen times, and on receiving a satisfactory answer, exclaiming, "*Al hamdu lillah*," "Praise be to God," in a tone of deep relief. We then sit down round the fire, and it might be imagined that the ceremony of welcome was at an end, but "not so, far otherwise than so." The same expressions are repeated over and over again, the new-comers addressing every one present in turn, and, as each volley of *selamáts* dies away, some one or other takes up the cue, and, as though he were uttering an entirely novel sentiment, exclaims, "*Selamát ya Mansúr.*" Even in the intervals of conversation which follow, the same remark is from time to time jerked out. The object of the old sheikh's presence was to demand a black-mail for our visit to his domain, and assert his right to a share in our camel hire; but both of these modest propositions we decisively negatived, and dismissed our visitor with a handful of coffee and our blessing.

As we were at work upon the inscriptions, a messenger from Suez passed us, and brought a letter calling Holland home. He at once prepared to obey the summons, and starting off on foot, with no other provision than a little bag of flour, reached Suez, a distance of some 110 miles, early in the afternoon of the third day, having walked the last forty miles without a rest; thus performing a pedestrian feat which has been rarely equalled, and the memory of which still lives in the country.

It was with no small emotion that I watched him out of sight, and found myself with no other companion but my trusty old Bedawí, Sálem. That worthy's grief on the occasion was profound and characteristic; he watched the retreating form for some minutes with an expression of incredulous amazement, and, when he had sufficiently realised the painful fact, applied his dirty sleeve to his eyes, and, sobbing outright, retired to hide his sorrow behind a neighbouring stone. After a few minutes he returned with red eyes and unwiped cheeks, and thus delivered himself: "God bless him! Four times has he been in this country, *and never cursed me once.*"

Making the best of my lonely situation, I applied myself with additional vigour to the task of copying and deciphering the inscriptions, and, having exhausted Wády Mukatteb, went down to Wády Igné (properly Gena), or, as it is sometimes called, Wády Maghárah, to examine the Egyptian mines and tablets there. It was indeed a day to make one realise the wilderness—alone with the barren rocks, and surrounded by works of industry interrupted or relinquished in patriarchal times, with the stiff conventional portraits of Pharaoh's ancestors looking down upon me from the wall. I sat and copied the inscriptions which recorded the might and conquests of the Egyptian king, and thought how much of unintentional sarcasm was contained in a speech made to me by Sálem the day before; "To-morrow we will copy Pharaoh in his pride." This, then, is what his pride has come to at last—his thousands of captive miners, his conquests and his wealth—a solitary traveller, three thousand years after, finishes him off with a note-book and a pipe.

The tablets are beautifully executed in bas-relief, and are of the usual familiar type; gigantic Pharaohs immolating diminutive captives, whose faces seem to express satisfaction at the honour of perishing by the royal hand; priests presenting offerings to hawk-headed divinities in attitudes which suggest boxing academies and the noble art of self-defence; troops of captives marching nowhere, and industriously chiselling nothing by the way; the background being occupied by hieroglyphic devices recording the exploits of the kings in whose reign the mines were worked.

Wády Igné is a narrow valley between two steep walls of sandstone, along the left-hand bank of which, as we ascend the wády, run a series of large caverns or galleries. The walls of these caverns, as well as the various fissures and cuttings in the rock, show chisel-marks which indicate the vast amount of labour expended on them. The instruments employed I believe to have been chisels of bronze or other hard metal, and not the flint flakes which are found in such quantities in the vicinity. The Egyptians, we know, were expert metallurgists, and flint implements could hardly have made such marks as those visible on the stone. The flints, if used at all, were probably employed in the sculpture of the hieroglyphic tablets; and this conjecture is confirmed by the fact that they are found in large numbers near the monuments of Sarábit el Khádim, but do not exist at the other Egyptian mines of Sinai, where no hieroglyphic tablets have been placed*. The mines were apparently worked for turquoises, as they are by the Arabs of the present day, who not unfrequently injure or destroy the sculptures by the too free use of blasting powder. It is probable also that some copper-ore may also have been found here, as in one place in the valley we found a small slag-heap and two cuttings on the vertical surface of a rock, which were evidently intended as moulds for running the metal into ingots. One of the tablets indeed mentions the

* These remarks were written on the spot, and before Mr Bauerman's communication to the Manchester Literary and Philosophical Society, in which that gentleman propounds a similar theory respecting the use of the flint implements.

"Goddess of Copper" as the presiding deity of the place.

As I returned to camp one evening, accompanied by the faithful Sâlem, we fell a-talking, as was our wont, upon the legendary associations of the country, and, having heard from him so many wondrous stories of "our Lord Moses" and the people of Israel, I in my turn told him the true history of the Exodus as it is written in the Inspired Word. He listened with rapt attention throughout the recital, only interrupting me now and then with a devout *Masha-'llah!* and, when I had finished, exclaimed, "By Heaven, these are beautiful words! why don't you tell the other gentlemen?" I explained that they all knew the history as well as I did, to which he merely replied sententiously, "Ah, but they can't understand it; *they don't know Arabic.*" Some of the old fellow's queer sayings are worthy to be put on record. On one occasion Captain Wilson returned from a mountain ascent, bringing with him a piece of coral which he had found upon the summit. This vastly puzzled old Sâlem, who justly remarked that "it was a sea affair, and had no business on a mountain top." We playfully explained to him that the world had been turned upside down, to which he replied in a solemn tone, "Ay, that it has, by the sins of wicked men."

After a week's work by myself, I was not sorry to hear the cheery voices of my companions, who had struck the camp at Feirân and come down to join me at Mukatteb. We had intended removing the tents to Maghárah as soon as our photographing was completed, but just then a fall of heavy rain made the roads too slippery for the camels, and we were consequently compelled to remain a few days longer on the spot. One afternoon, between the showers, Captain Wilson and I went down to the bilingual inscription which I have before mentioned, in order to ascertain if it were possible to remove it uninjured by blasting the rock beneath it, since the Arabs had failed in cutting it out, owing to the want of proper tools and the hardness of the stone. While examining the rock for this purpose, we pointed out to one of the Arabs the figure of a camel among the inscriptions. He regarded it with intense delight and astonishment, declaring that his father and grandfather had lived all their lives in the country, and had never seen such a thing before; and yet similar figures occur in numbers wherever there are inscriptions on the rocks. Another Arab, who had been sent for a fuze, now came up, and was informed by his companions of the wonderful discovery. He sat down before the stone pointed out to him, and peered for some moments at the figure with a vacant and bewildered stare, when suddenly the light dawned upon him, and he uttered a howl of childish delight, which resounded through the valley and threw us into fits of laughter. The Bedawín are certainly not remarkable for habits of close observation: it was only a day or so before that Captain Palmer and I were admiring a lovely sunset effect, when an Arab near us halted, stared vaguely into space, and asked us what we were looking at! On another occasion, as I stood in Wády 'Ajeleh and gazed at the noble peak of Jebel el Benát, which was then bathed in a glorious crimson light, I involuntarily remarked to Sálem my companion, "How beautiful that mountain looks!" "Oh no!" he replied, "it's not at all beautiful—it's very hard to climb!"

When all was ready we applied the fuze, but the rock burst away so dangerously near to the inscription, that we dared not repeat the experiment, and were reluctantly compelled to relinquish the attempt and content ourselves with a plaster cast of this most interesting monument. For the guidance of future antiquaries, I may mention that a stone platform which stands in front of this inscription, has no connection whatever with the worship of Baal, having been erected with great labour by Mr Holland to facilitate our working at the stone.

In the evening of the same day we were visited by an outlaw, who sought the shelter of our camp. He had struck a man with his sword, under circumstances of great provocation, the blow had proved fatal, and he was now flying from the *thár* or "blood revenge," travelling over the mountains all the way in order to avoid the public road. Such a life must be a more deterrent example than even the gallows, and its effects are visible in the fact that human life is more respected by the Arabs than by any other nation in the world. The Bedawín know no distinction between murder and homicide, and the stern provision of the ancient law has still full force among the sons of Ishmael, "Whoso sheddeth man's blood, by man shall his blood be shed."

On reaching Wády Igné, our first visit was to the dwelling of the late Major Macdonald, an English officer, who, tempted by the exaggerated accounts of the wealth of the turquoise mines, took up his abode in the wilderness, and employed the Arabs in searching for the precious stones. They turned out to be of little or no commercial value; and, after passing some years in his self-imposed exile, he returned to Egypt, where he died a ruined and disappointed man.

He had selected a sheltered spot in the immediate neighbourhood of the mines, and, having levelled the ground and removed all obstructing rocks by blasting or cutting them away, had built himself a rude but commodious house. In front is a pleasant terrace whereon to take the air, and just below this are the kitchen and other offices, and a plot of ground laid out for gardening purposes. A path, too, has been made for camels and foot-passengers to the spring about a mile distant, and to the summit of the neighbouring hill. Near the spot we found the remains of "Blackie," the Major's cat—some hair and teeth were all that was left to tell of the poor desert puss. When inhabited and kept in order, the house must have looked pretty and picturesque, but it is now in a very deserted and dilapidated state, and is used as a storehouse by the Arabs. Behind it is a low mountain of sandstone, the summit of which consists of a rounded peak set upon a flat plateau and commanding a view of the whole of the opposite mines. This plateau is covered with the ruins of small stone huts, and was no doubt occupied by the captive miners and their military guardians. Crossing the wády a little higher up is a broad line of stones, which has been mistaken for a wall, but is evidently the remains of a causeway by which the gangs of miners were driven to and from their work. From this hill we observed some cuttings in the opposite rocks, at a considerable distance above the other mines; and, as the Arabs reported that they contained hieroglyphic tablets, we descended into the valley and made straight for them. Owing to their height and the treacherous nature of the sandstone, we did not reach them without considerable difficulty and some danger, but were rewarded by the discovery of two tablets in an excellent state of preservation. The lower of these is cut upon the flat vertical surface of a rock, and represents a group of miners at work, superintended by a soldier armed with a bow and arrow, the prototype of the present Egyptian police-officer, who is still called a *cawwás*, or archer. This tablet is exceedingly interesting, as it shows the form of tools employed in working the mines. These consist of a chisel of the ordinary pattern, and a kind of swivel hammer, which would seem to have been used by placing the heavy part upon the ground, and working it from the handle. The hammer itself was probably of greenstone, many such being found

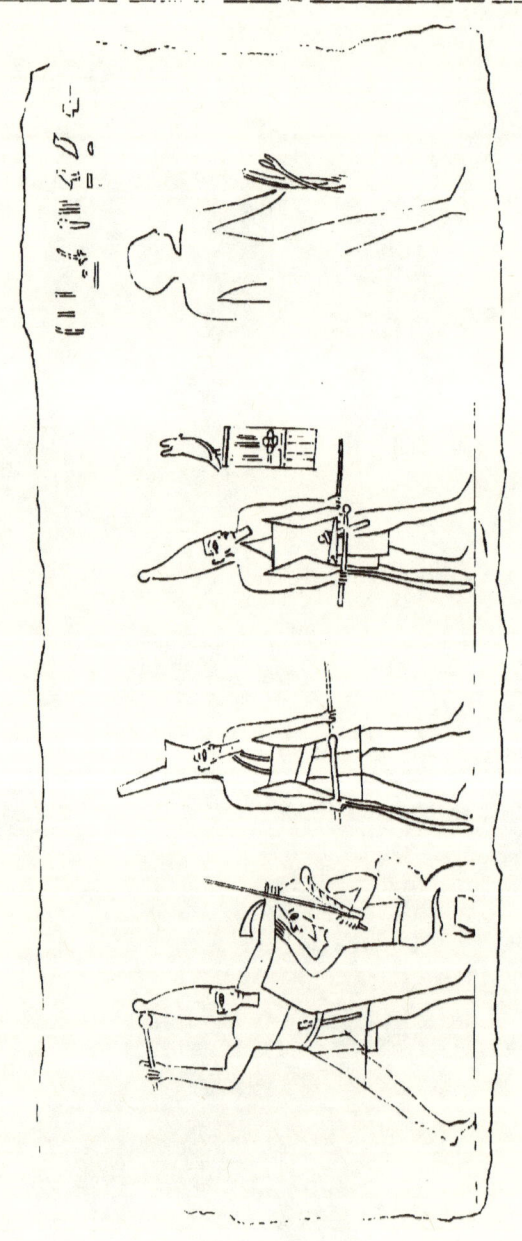

EGYPTIAN TABLET AT MAGHARAH

in the neighbourhood of the excavations. The handle is half the length of the rest or stem; lower down, in the galleries ordinarily visited, we found what was evidently a rough representation of the same tool.

The second tablet was upon the walls of a cave, the rock in front of which had given way, and, as we hesitated even in the interests of science to trust ourselves to a projection of crumbling sandstone at a height of nearly eighty feet on a sheer precipice, we were not able to obtain a "squeeze" impression of it. On the hills opposite the mines and near the mouth of the valley we also found a tablet hitherto unknown. It was executed in bas-relief on a flat ledge of rock, and represented a miner of the period taking the air with his wife and son. Its style was much ruder than that of the official hieroglyphs by the mines themselves, and it had evidently been cut by one of the Egyptian artists to beguile a leisure hour.

As well as the hieroglyphics there are several Greek and Sinaitic inscriptions amongst the mines, and these are for the most part cut with a chisel, and not dotted in with sharp stones, showing that some at least of the writers of the inscriptions were predecessors of Major Macdonald on this antiquarian Tom Tiddler's ground.

One instance of this is very instructive, as it completely demolishes the theory which ascribes an Israelitish origin to these Aramæan scrawls. To the philologist this theory needs no disproof, but, as the well-meant but mistaken enthusiasm of the author of "Sinai Photographed" may still mislead the unlearned and credulous, I shall perhaps be pardoned for discussing the question here. Unsound and absurd as the arguments of that book are, it is but due to the author to say that he writes as an earnest Christian gentleman who himself believes in what he asserts, and it is much to be regretted that a life's labour should be so lost. In the above-mentioned work one of the tablets is described as bilingual, with contemporaneous inscriptions in Egyptian and Sinaitic characters, a photograph taken from a paper impression being inserted by way of illustration. The "Sinaitic text" is followed by what is called "the living and breathing figure of an ostrich;" to this, as "the symbol of the Children of Israel," the inscription is made to refer, the grammar and vocabulary used in the interpretation being *perfectly unique*. In reality, the tablet is an Egyptian one, consisting of a series of three cut surfaces, the last unfinished. On this temptingly smooth face a Greek has written an inscription, of which time has defaced all but a few letters, and *over this* is chiselled a comparatively recent Sinaitic inscription. The ostrich turns out to be a slip of the chisel flaking off a piece of the smoothed surface of the stone. I could multiply instances of this sort, but do not care to break a butterfly upon the wheel.

Not far from the mines is a small wády called Umm Themáïn, which runs into the Seih Sidreh, the debouchure of the wádies Mukatteb, Sidreh and Igné. Here, we were told, might be seen a mysterious cave, of which the Arabs could give no other account than that it was full of bats and very extensive. This cave Captain Wilson and I determined to explore, and having found the mouth, some little distance up the hill-side, we proceeded to divest ourselves of our outer clothing, and, taking lighted candles in our hand and one end of a large ball of string as a clue, entered the small, dark opening. We crept serpent-wise along narrow, winding galleries for about four hundred feet, and still found other passages to explore. The air was hot and stifling, bats flew out with shrill and startled screams, and festooned themselves upon our hair and beards; the walls were black with the smoke of lamps, extinct, like their owners' lives, long ages ago, and in one place, where a small side cutting had been made, the miners had propped up the roof with a branch of shittim wood. There it stood, dry and brown enough certainly, but as perfect in shape as when it was first set up, perhaps before the Great Pyramid was built. That these mines, like the others, are Egyptian is proved by the existence of two hieroglyphic tablets in the valley beneath, and their age may be imagined when we reflect that, while those at Wády Igné close by, which are certainly as old as Cheops, are in excellent preservation, these are so time-worn as to be perfectly illegible, only a few stray hieroglyphs remaining to tell of what they were. We were unable to conjecture what could have been the object of the miners, as no trace could be discovered either of metal or turquoise veins.

The special survey of Serbál being completed, and Wády Mukatteb and Maghárah carefully examined and photographed, we began a more general reconnaissance of the routes of the Peninsula. But the description of these wanderings must be reserved for another chapter.

CHAPTER XI.

WANDERINGS IN THE WILDERNESS.

Desert shore of the Red Sea. Wády Dhaghadeh. A mud bath. The Plain of El Gá'ah. Wády Sigillíyeh. Beautiful landscape effects. We explore an unknown gorge, and take to the water; horror of old Sálem. Another desert walk. The Mirage. Abu Suweirah. Jebel Nágús; curious acoustic phenomenon; legend of the origin of the sound. Moses' Hot-bath. Excavated chapels. The village of Tor. Wády Hebrán. More primeval dwellings. Head of Wády Sigillíyeh. Ruined Convents. Wady Feirán. An Arab strike.

A DREARIER walk than that from the mines in Wády Igné to the coast of the Red Sea can scarcely be imagined. Leaving on our right the Nagb Buderah, the pass by which travellers from Egypt usually approach Mukatteb, we followed the course of the Seih Sidreh, past monotonous banks of cretaceous conglomerate, which, becoming gradually lower and lower, lose themselves at last in the general level of the sandy plain, and by noon on the second day we found ourselves on the sea-shore.

Familiar as we had grown with desert scenes, we were not prepared for such utter and oppressive desolation as this; the blue waters lay calm or rather dead before us, a realisation of the "Ancient Mariner's" dreary vision, whilst on either hand, as far as eye could reach, there stretched a dull flat sandy waste, unrelieved by any green or living thing—the barren wilderness and the still more "sterile sea" side by side. It was as though nature had left this spot to point out to man how awful indeed were the fulfilment of the ancient sentence, "Cursed is the ground for thy sake," did not her bounteous and regenerating hand temper the dreadful doom.

A walk of sixteen miles over yielding sand, beneath a scorching sun, is not interesting either to perform or describe, and the task of writing our journals when we reached our camp at the mouth of the Wády Feirán was therefore not a long one. The next morning we again set out, and passed over a tract of sand equally dreary with that of the day before, but, being covered with a sombre carpet of hard, black flints, it afforded a firmer foothold for the pedestrian. The sun shone with a fierce glare, scorching and blistering our hands and faces; and, as there was not a particle of shade to be had, we were fain to trudge on wearily all day without our customary halt or lunch, for to have rested without shelter would have inevitably entailed sun-stroke or roasting alive.

At last, to our delight, we reached the mouth of a small wády called Dhaghadeh, a lovely valley through which ran a clear, cool stream bordered by a grove of palm-trees; on these the dead branches hung in many a graceful and fantastic shape, and their colour contrasted prettily with the bright green of the feathery young leaves.

After such heat and fatigue as we had recently undergone, the water was too tempting, and Captain Wilson and I were soon enjoying, as far as myriads of sand-flies would permit us to, a dip in a tiny pool. Our bath was more remarkable, however, for its refreshing than for its detergent effects, since it had a bottom of soft, black mud.

As we strolled back to camp, there darted up from under our very feet a large snake, with a flat venomous head and a wicked whip-like tail. Science whispered, "Catch him alive," and suggested pickle-bottles and alcohol; but prudence urged, "Stand back and let somebody kill him," and I flatter myself I am not an imprudent man. Old Sálem quickly appeared upon the scene in answer to my summons, and after he had made a vigorous assault upon it with stones we regarded complacently its scaly and mangled corpse.

In the morning we proceeded a short distance up the wády, and mounted a projecting shoulder of the mountain which promised a commanding view of the surrounding district. The landscape was novel and picturesque: we looked down upon a large amphitheatre of sandstone hills, broken up into numberless little jagged peaks which gleamed in the sunlight with bright and vivid hues like the minarets of some fairy city of Eastern romance.

Above this variegated wall rose the majestic mass of Serbál, and the smaller but no less beautiful mountain of Umm Lahm. All around, the hills were intersected by labyrinthine torrent-courses, a grove of palm-trees lining the main bed of the valley, and a gentle stream flowing past their stems added greatly to the beauty of the scene. From this inviting spot we retraced our steps, and, braving once more the burning plain, set out for the adjacent valley, Wády Sigillíyeh, which we had determined to explore, and at the mouth of which our Arabs had been told to pitch the tents. This plain is a flat and arid strip of desert which stretches from the base of the Sinai mountains down to the sea, and extends along the whole of the south-western coast of the Peninsula. It is called emphatically El Gá'ah, or "the Plain"; and, although it does not quite answer to the description given by Burckhardt that "it is so flat that water will not run upon it," it is perhaps one of the most uncompromising pieces of desert of which Arabia can boast. For an hour and a half we plodded on without meeting with a single object to relieve the monotony of our walk; but at the expiration of that time we reached a solitary shittim or acacia tree, which afforded a few feet of shade, and, regardless of the long stiletto-like thorns that strewed the ground beneath it, we threw ourselves at full length on the sand and enjoyed a slight repose and slighter lunch. Two hours more of sun and sand brought us to our tents, which were pitched in the Seil Sigillíyeh, the debouchure of the system of valleys which drains the southern face of Serbâl. The situation was bleak and uncomfortable; on the one hand lay the desolate expanse of desert, skirted by a low range of featureless hills which effectually concealed the sea from our view; on the other rose a mighty granite wall, broken only by a narrow gorge which forms the outlet for the waters of Sigillíyeh.

This gorge was declared by the Arabs to be quite impassable, and we were therefore compelled on the following morning to seek an entrance into the valley by a pass leading over one of the lower mountains, which form as it were the outposts of the group. From this we descended into a lovely glen, between precipitous cliffs, and paved with smooth white granite; along this there flowed a murmuring stream, which ever and anon, as it trickled over some larger rocks, formed itself into a deep pool or tiny waterfall, overshadowed by fantastic rocks and graced with ferns and desert herbage of the richest green.

It is these sudden glimpses of scenery, these unexpected transitions from monotonous sterility to grand landscape and exuberant vegetation, which impart so great a charm to desert travel.

Our object was to reach, if possible, the ruins of an ancient convent on the slopes of Jebel Sigillíyeh itself; but as we found, after walking some eight miles or so, that the mountain was still a long way off, we deemed it prudent to defer our visit and approach the ruins on some future occasion from the upper end of the valley; halting, therefore, beneath some shady rocks which overhung a pool of clear cold water, we prepared, after a short rest, to retrace our steps. The valley, from its mouth to a point some distance up where it is joined by a tributary from the neighbouring mountain of Umm Lahm, is called Jebáah, and after this takes the name of Sigillíych. It drains the whole seaward front of the immense Serbál cluster; and the water-worn appearance of its granite floor, and the rugged devastation that characterize it, testify to the immense volumes of water that at certain times and seasons pour through the valley. The Arabs declare that, when there are *seils*, or "floods," the narrow gorge through which the wády debouches is sometimes filled from top to bottom with the torrent, a depth of more than four hundred feet; and the polished walls of the cleft, and the positions of the immense boulders which block up its entrance, certainly lend countenance to their statement. Wishing to examine the spot thoroughly, we determined to return by the chasm, instead of by the pass over which we had entered the wády, and turned a deaf ear to the vehement assertions of our Bedawín guides, who declared that it was dangerous and impracticable. Casting a farewell glance up the valley, the scene presented to our view was, if possible, more wild and wondrous than before. Mountain walls towered up sheer and precipitous on either side; huge boulders of rock either bordered the course of the stream, or obstructing it, formed falls, with little pools beneath; tall wavy rushes with feathery heads grew to the height of twelve or fourteen feet, at intervals along the way; grasshoppers, dragon-flies, and locusts of gigantic size (*jikhdiz*) skimmed around; the glittering gravel was marked with innumerable tracks of beasts that shun the haunts of men, from the small cloven hoof of the ibex to the huge round leopard's paw; partridges rose whirring from beneath our feet at every step; —and yet, with all these signs of life, there was an air of lone but lovely desolation all around. No European, the Arabs declared, had ever visited the place before; and even of our own escort no one could be found who knew the way except a little boy, Freih, who had once upon an emergency been sent to find his way across the mountains from Feirán to Tor, and had chosen this very road.

The sun was already sinking as we prepared to essay the passage of the mysterious gorge. The first glance did not reveal an inviting prospect, for on one side rose a perpendicular wall of granite to a height of about fifteen hundred feet, and on the other a rock some thirty feet high, as smooth as though it had been polished by a lapidary's hand. Between them was a pool of water, breast deep on one side, and about twelve feet on the other, and the only means of entering this were, on the shallow side by stepping upon a heap of stones, and on the other by a plunge. Captain Palmer managed to scramble barefoot up the slippery rock, and, being taller, let himself down, at some risk, on the other side of the pool, while Captain Wilson and I prepared to take to the water. Old Sálem had seated himself, with a complacent smile, until we should come to a more rational frame of mind, but at this stage of the proceedings he became frantic in his remonstrance, and was with some difficulty persuaded to hand us on our clothes. "For heaven's sake, don't go in there!" he exclaimed. "It's over your heads." "*Ma lish*, Never mind," said we: "What, never mind, when it's over your head?" old Sálem replied, and sitting down he groaned aloud, conducting himself like a prudent-minded hen who sees her brood of ducklings taking to a pond. When we had reached the other side, he packed up his things with a deep sigh and prepared to go back to camp by the way we came. "Ah, Sálem," I cried, "you never left us in the lurch before!" "Never!" he replied, stung to the quick by the reproach; and rushing wildly at the rock, he selected the steepest and most impracticable part, and proceeded to make vain and frantic efforts, determining either to walk up the sides or perish in the attempt. He was about successfully to accomplish the latter feat, when, seeing that he was really distressed, we explained that we had only been laughing at him, and allowed him to seek the safer road over the mountain pass. Our next step was as difficult as the first; but here the water was inaccessible, and the rock ended in an abrupt drop of about fifteen feet.

Sliding down to the edge of this, we stuck on as well as we could, and reflected upon the best course to pursue, until at last Palmer, with a desperate effort, let himself go, and saving Wilson as best he could, they rolled over in a heap at the bottom, where they formed themselves into an obelisk and caught me on the top. Making a run over a smooth and narrow sloping ledge, which overhung an unpleasant precipice, we reached a flat piece of rock; but, just as we were congratulating ourselves upon having mastered all our difficulties, we found that this terminated abruptly in a yawning chasm about two hundred feet in depth, with water at the bottom. Our chance of reaching camp that night appeared a very doubtful one, as the sun had already dipped behind the hills, and in a few minutes more it would be dark; and to get back again, even if there were light enough, was simply impossible. At last, however, we discovered a kind of broken path, apparently an attempt in former times to reach the higher pools from the mouth of the gorge, and scrambling along it, we emerged at length into the open country, where we were received by our Arabs with enthusiastic congratulations on our escape from the mysterious ravine which human eyes had never before explored. Until a late hour that night we heard old Sálem narrating over the camp fire how the Khawáját swam through huge lakes and mounted slippery precipices "by making ladders of themselves," and how they were as mad as mad could be!

Early in the morning we set off to cross El Gá'ah to the sea-coast. Another dreary prospect awaited us; for twenty miles there lay before us a bare plain of gravel, without a single tree or stone upon it that might afford a shelter from the sun, which gave every promise of a broiling day. For ten miles we walked on, the heat and glare becoming every moment more insupportable; at last, finding a small bush about two feet high, we sat down, and hiding our heads, like the traditional ostrich, in its shade, enjoyed a few minutes' rest and a pipe. On our way across the plain we witnessed a striking instance of the phenomenon of *mirage*. Some distance away on our left appeared a huge lake of clear and rippling water; rows of large trees were growing by its side, and their shadows being reflected on the surface wore a strange semblance of reality. Some Arabs riding on camels passed the spot and their shadows, also lengthened in the sunlight, fell upon the surface of the lake; one of them dismounted and sat down upon the ground while his beast cropped some parched desert herb, and this completed the illusion. We could with difficulty persuade ourselves that the clear inviting expanse was nothing but a tremulous vapour, and that the noble trees upon its banks were only stunted shrubs. The reality was even more vivid than I had been led to expect from the descriptions which I had read of this curious phenomenon; unlike the *ignis fatuus*, it does not appear to recede from you as you approach, and it is only when you are comparatively close upon it that it begins to fade away and the real cause of the illusion is revealed, a sort of transparent mist such as may be seen any day by holding a flame between the eye and the bright sunlight.

At last we reached the base of the hills which skirt the plain, and passing through a narrow defile found ourselves on the shore of the Red Sea. The place which we had selected for our camp was a pleasant little palm-grove, called Abu Suweirah, and the cool green of the trees was most refreshing to the eye after the yellow glare of the desert.

On the opposite African coast the sun was just setting behind the grand solitary mountain of El 'Akráb, and shed a stream of golden light across the azure waters, while the murmur of the waves, which washed up almost to the door of our tents, fell gratefully upon our ear and whispered of baths, *narghilehs*, and perfect *kif*, to which we had long been strangers. Taking the hint, we braved the sharks and bathed our weary limbs before dinner, after which we lay upon the beach and smoked *narghilehs* beneath the melancholy moon.

Our first care the next morning was to visit Jebel Nágús, the object which had brought us to this part of the country. This mountain receives its name from certain curious sounds which proceed from it, and which are supposed to resemble those of a *nágús*, that is, of the wooden gong used in Eastern churches in lieu of bells. It is situated at about three-quarters of a mile from the sea-coast, and forms the north-western extremity of the range of hills which we had just crossed to our camp at Abu Suweirah. The mountain itself is composed of white friable sandstone, and filling a large gully in the side facing west-southwest, is a slope of fine drift sand about 380 feet in height, eighty yards wide at the base, and tapering towards the top, where it branches off into three or four narrow gullies. The sand lies at so high an angle to the horizon, nearly 30°, and is so fine and dry, as to be easily set in motion from any point in the slope, or even by scraping away a portion from its base. When this is done, the sand rolls down with a sluggish viscous motion, and it is then that the sound begins, at first a low vibratory moan, but gradually swelling out into a roar like thunder, and as gradually dying away again, until the sand has ceased to roll. To me the sound seemed more like that caused by air entering the mouth of a large metal vessel, and I could produce an imitation of it on a small scale by turning my flask at a certain angle to the wind. We found that the heated surface was much more sensitive to sound than the cooler layers beneath, and that those parts of the slope which had laid long undisturbed, produced a much louder and more lasting sound than those which had recently been set in motion, thus showing that the phenomenon is purely local and superficial, and due in some manner to the combined effects of heat and friction. A faint sound could also be produced by sweeping portions of the sand rapidly forward with the arm; and this caused such a peculiar tingling sensation in the operator's arm as to suggest that some electrical influence was also at work. When a large quantity of the sand was set in motion and the sound was at its height a powerful vibration was felt, and straws stuck into the sand trembled visibly although there was not a breath of wind to disturb them. The sand on the upper part of the slope where it branches off into the gullies above mentioned is coarser and more adulterated with extraneous particles, *detritus* from the overhanging rocks and pieces of seaweed blown up from the shore; it is consequently less easily set in motion, and we found it to be much less sensitive to sound. The inclination of the slope is the "angle of rest" of the sand in its normal state; but excessive heat or drought, wind, animals running over the slope, falling rocks and many other accidents might act as disturbing causes; in any of these cases the sound would occur, and its spontaneous production, which has caused so much speculation, may be therefore easily accounted for. Besides the large slide there is a narrow slope to the north; and part of this, being in shade the whole day long during the winter months, afforded us an opportunity of determining the comparative sensitiveness of the heated and cool sand. We found that the sand on the cool, shaded portion, at a temperature of 62° produced but a very faint sound when set in motion; while that on the more exposed parts, at a temperature of 103° gave forth a loud and often even startling noise. Other sand-slopes in the vicinity were also experimented upon, but these which were composed of coarser grains and inclined at a lower angle produced no acoustic phenomena whatever. The Arabs declare that the sounds are only heard on Fridays and Sundays, and tell the following legend respecting their origin :—

An Arab, whose people were encamped by the palm-grove of Abu Suweirah, happened to stroll alone by the sea-shore, and coming to the spot in question, which he had hitherto believed to be barren and uninhabited, he was surprised to find a small monastery and a pleasant garden on the mountain side. The brethren received him courteously, and invited him to partake of their meal, to which, being hungry and fatigued, he gladly consented. Having shared their hospitality, he prepared to depart, but first, at the instance of his hosts, he took a solemn oath that he would never reveal to any living soul the secret of their retreat or of his own meeting with them. He was accompanied for a portion of his way home by two of the monks, who reiterated their injunctions of secrecy and took their leave. The Arab, however, prompted either by curiosity or baser motives, took the opportunity of dropping the stones of some dates which he had eaten, in order that he might have a clue by which to find the place again; and on reaching the tents of his tribe he at once related his adventure, regardless alike of his oath and of the sacred laws of hospitality. His people refused to credit his account until he offered to conduct them himself to the place; but, when he attempted to do this, he found that all the date-stones had been removed. He did, however, succeed in identifying the mountain, but the monastery, gardens, and monks had all disappeared, and nothing remained to show that they had ever existed save the sound of the *náyús* calling them to prayers within their mysterious retreat in the very heart of the mountain. The Arab who had thus disregarded the sacred obligations of bread and salt, not only forfeited the esteem of his own people, but misfortune after misfortune overtook him until he perished miserably, an outcast from his fellow-men.

The next morning I walked down by the shore towards the village of Tor, picking my way over the jagged limestone spurs, masses of fossil corals jutting out into the sea, until I reached the mountain which is described in the maps by the ill-omened name of Jebel Himám, or "The Mount of Death." This name, I found, like many others, has been inaccurately reported by previous travellers—the real appellation being Jebel Hammám, "The Mountain of the Hot-bath;" and my authorities for this correction, two ragged Arab urchins, then and there conducted me to Hammám Syedná Músa, "Our Lord Moses' bath," in proof of their statements. I found it to consist of a natural hot spring, which takes its rise in the mountain, and trickles down by various canals into the midst of a large palm-grove belonging to the monastery of St Katharine. A series of chambers, similar in construction and arrangement to those of an ordinary Turkish bath, have been built over it for the convenience of those who take its waters; these being strongly impregnated with sulphur, as well as of an extremely high temperature, are considered very beneficial in certain forms of disease. Here I met Sálem, whom I had sent on to Tor for a guide, and who now, after making friends with the "oldest inhabitant," returned brimful of importance and information. He had been told of some curious "houses in the rock" in the hills behind our camp, and for these we at once set out.

They proved to be a series of Christian chapels excavated in the rock, with a few hermits' cells attached; in several the plaster still adhered to the walls, and this was covered with rude crosses in red paint, and a few pious inscriptions in Greek and Armenian. From these and numerous other remains which we met with in the neighbourhood, it is evident that Tor must have been a place of considerable importance during the early monkish occupation of the Peninsula, and it is more than probable that all the stores, and a great portion of the pilgrims, in the middle ages reached Sinai from this direction. The present village of Tor is a wretched little hamlet, consisting of a few fishermen's huts; the requirements of the convent still connect it with Suez by a very small traffic, and an agent of the monks resides there to superintend their extensive date-groves. The few families of the place are Christians, and occasionally make short pilgrimages to Mount Sinai, where I have frequently met them in the convent church. The climate of Tor is very unhealthy, and owing to the low and marshy nature of the ground there is a great deal of miasma even in the winter season. We ourselves soon began to experience its effects, and were glad once more to exchange such an unwholesome atmosphere for the bracing air of the mountains.

I shall spare my readers a description of our second walk across El Gá'ah on our way back, as I find, on comparing my notes with those of my companions on the occasion, that the only incident recorded by any of us during the day was the discovery of one stunted shittim-tree in the middle of the plain.

This time we struck across rather more to the east, and entered the mountains by Wády Hebrán. It is a narrow winding valley, containing a perennial stream and two projecting rocks of a very remarkable shape; the scenery is not so picturesque as that of Sigillíyeh, but the valley is nevertheless imposing in the rude grandeur of its features. A road was commenced from Tor to Sinai *viâ* Wády Hebrán by the late 'Abbás Pasha, but it was never completed; some portions have still survived neglect and the destructive effects of the floods. At the watershed of the wády is an enormous collection of those primitive dwellings, called *nawámís*, which I have before had occasion to describe.

After crossing the pass, and enjoying from thence a grand view of the rugged peaks of Serbál and its neighbouring mountains, we descended into Wády er Rimm, a valley falling into the great trunk wády immediately above Feirán, and turned aside to find a convenient camping ground, from whence we might visit the ruins of Sigillíyeh, which we had failed to reach from the other side. Here we found an encampment of Feirán Arabs, many of whom were personally known to us, and who greeted us after our absence with an unfeigned cordiality that made our return amongst these children of the desert seem almost like a welcome home. I have seen a great deal of Arab life and character since my sojourn in Sinai, but amongst no other tribe of Bedawín have I met with so much honour, good feeling, and simplicity as amongst the poor Towarah.

Early the next morning we started on our proposed excursion. A camel-road once led up to the monastic retreat, but of this time and frequent floods have now destroyed almost every trace, and our walk up Wády er Rimm would have been trying to the best-shod pedestrian; it was especially so to me, whose boots had come to so deplorable a pass that I was fain to tie them on my feet with my pocket-handkerchief. When we had reached the highest point, a grand and impressive landscape met our view. On the left a stately rock towered high into the air above our heads, so sheer and precipitous that one might almost have dropped a plumb-line from the summit into the valley, some twelve hundred feet below. Behind us was a huge smooth peak, Jebel Shinónír, the easternmost portion of Serbál; forming, as it were, the buttress of that majestic pile. Our only way down into the valley was by a steep and awkward-looking slide, or rather ravine filled with boulders, loose stones, and treacherous gravel *jorfs*; the gradient was so steep that a boulder kicked from the top bounded down without impediment amid an awful roar and clouds of dust to the very bottom of the gully. Just before us, and at right angles to our path, ran the Wády Sigillíyeh, though nothing more could be seen of it than the commencement of its rugged floor and the broad plateau on its eastern side split into a hundred dells and rough ravines. On the watershed, where we stood, were some old stone ruins, a hermit's deserted cell, and a leopard-trap, in front of which were recent traces of a huge beast of that species.

After a few yards of loose gravel, we came upon a portion of the old road, composed of large blocks of granite arranged as a flight of steps; but this presently terminated in an abrupt precipice, where the floods had broken away the ground, and it was at least half an hour before we could find a practicable path. Arrived at the bottom, we found another admirably constructed road, quite a model of engineering skill, which ran along the shoulder of the opposite mountain, and shortly brought us to our destination. Here we stood upon the brow of a hill looking down into a deep ravine filled with palms and other trees, indicating the presence of a living stream of water; and amidst the verdure were the walls of a small convent, the ruins which we were seeking. Descending into the ravine we made a careful examination of these, and then partially retracing our steps we went out on to a projecting spur of the hill, and found behind it another glen, still wilder and more beautiful than that which we had left, and also filled with ruined monkish dwellings and garden walls. Looking across the wády, too, we saw a third ravine with palm-trees and tall rushes peeping above its winding walls, and evidently containing similar dwellings to those beneath us, since the road along the mountain side leading to it, was the counterpart of that by which we ourselves had reached the ruins. Southward was the Wády Sigillíyeh ; far away in the distance could be seen the narrow gorge whose difficulties we had so recently experienced, and beyond this stretched the burning plain of El Gá'ah. A more wildly picturesque and secluded retreat than this it would be difficult to conceive, and with the luxuriant vegetation that fills the wády-bed, and the almost inaccessible nature of the place, it forms the very ideal of a Bedawí "Happy Vale." Judging from the fact that we found numerous Sinaitic inscriptions at the bottom of the pass in Wády er Rimm, that is, as far as camels could have been brought when the roads were better kept, and none at all after the part at which the real difficulties of the ascent commence, I should conclude that the Saracen carriers gave in at this point, allowing the worthy monks to fetch their stores over the mountains, and occupied themselves in the interval by carving their autographs upon the rocks, since no other mischief was left for their idle hands to do. Having had our fill of reflection and admiration, we returned towards camp, which we reached by moonlight, tired and well-nigh exhausted by the, even to us, unwonted fatigues of the day.

About one o'clock the next day we had walked over the nine miles which separated us from our old camp at Feirán, and were soon sitting on the floor of the mess-tent, eating sardines. We found that the Arab population whom we employed in carrying the instruments, and other odd jobs, had risen in our absence against the sergeant's sway, and struck for higher wages. They had even gone so far as to declare that we should not employ old Sálem, a Sh'oeibí Arab, any longer, but must take one of their own number in his stead; and they had actually threatened Hisán, our Serbál guide, with personal violence if he ventured to work for us again until the question was settled. This incipient Semitic Broadheadism I at once nipped in the bud by forbidding the Feirán Arabs to come near our tents, and telling them that Sálem and Hisán were *dakhíls* of the Expedition, that is, under our sworn protection, and that we should consider any injury or annoyance to them as if it had been offered to ourselves. My plan had the desired effect of at once repressing the outbreak; the ringleaders of the movement overwhelmed us with apologies and explanations, and thus ended the "strike at Feirán," without a single bottle of explosive mixture being thrown into our tents. But then the Arabs have not the advantages of education and civilisation like their fellow-sufferers of Sheffield in Christian England, and I must beg the patrons of rattening and similar philanthropists, should these pages meet their eye, to make some allowance on this score for the poor Bedawín's utter indifference to "the rights of the working man."

CHAPTER XII.

THE HIGHWAYS AND BYWAYS OF SINAI.

Return to Mukatteb and Maghárah. Wády Sidreh. Sarábít el Khádim, Egyptian remains; their origin and purport; mines. Wády Nasb. Wády Bab'a; plague of insects. Plain of El Markhá. Abu Zenímeh. Wády Taiyebeh; Encampment by the Red Sea. Wádies Ethál and Useit. Hammám Far'ún; hot springs; legend of Pharaoh's bath; a hurricane. Jebel Músa again.

A FEW days sufficed us to rest and "post up" our back work, after which we again got into marching order and resumed our wanderings in the highways and byways of the Peninsula. We first of all proceeded to pay another visit to Wády Mukatteb, taking with us Sergeant Macdonald, the photographer of the Expedition, and obtained some excellent photographs of the inscriptions and of the neighbouring mines in Wády Igné. As our journey thus far lay unavoidably over the same ground which we had before travelled, there was little or nothing left to note or remark upon our way. Hence we struck up Wády Sidreh, a narrow valley falling into Mukatteb

on the right, intending to cross over into Sarábít el
Khádim. This valley, which had never before been
explored, winds up into the mountains for about two
hours, and after this turns off into a broad open
wády, called Umm Ajráf, which is again joined by
Wády Khamílch, on the road from Suez to Jebel
Músa. From this place to Sarábít our path lay
over the same piece of road as that which we had
travelled on our first entry into the country, namely,
over the rough pass of Súwig to the mouth of Wády
Sarábít itself, where we encamped as near as possible to the foot of the mountain. Although only
seven hundred feet in height, the ascent of Sarábít
el Khádim is by no means easy. A scramble over a
rough slide of loose sandstone at the upper end of
the valley, a treacherous sloping ledge of rock overhanging an awkward precipice, and a steep ravine
which brings into play all one's gymnastic capabilities, leads to an extensive plateau broken up by
many deep ravines and rising knolls. On one of the
highest of these last is a heap of ruins—hewn sandstone walls, with broken columns, and numerous *stelæ*,
in shape like ordinary English gravestones, standing
or scattered at irregular intervals about the place,
the whole being surrounded by the *débris* of an outer
wall. The buildings consist of two temples, apparently of different dates—one constructed entirely
of hewn stones, the other formed by two chambers
excavated in the rock at the easternmost end, and
having a walled continuation in front. In the largest
of these chambers the walls show signs of having

been once completely covered with hieroglyphics, though a great portion have now scaled off; at the upper end is a small niche, probably the altar, beside which is a carved figure in bas-relief. Another niche is seen at the right-hand corner, and in the centre of the chamber is a pillar, cut in the solid rock and covered with hieroglyphics. Some of the hieroglyphics in this cave still bear traces of the paint with which they were formerly ornamented, emerald green inside the characters, with a red and black band above and below. The cornice of the wall which forms the continuation of the temple is ornamented with a pretty pattern, and fragments of Egyptian coping lie around the entrance. The *stelæ* above mentioned, as well as such of the walls of the building as are still left standing, are also covered with hieroglyphics, and amongst them may be remarked the *cartouches* of many of the earliest Egyptian kings. The purpose of these monuments was for a long time enveloped in mystery, but the researches of Professor Lepsius and other learned Egyptologists have shown that they were connected with the working of copper mines in the neighbourhood, and that the temple was probably that in which the miners and their guards worshipped the national gods of Egypt. The mines themselves were first re-discovered by Mr Holland, during a previous visit to the Peninsula, and were carefully examined by the Expedition on this occasion; they exist in great numbers in the neighbourhood of the temple, and several of them contain beautifully executed hieroglyphic tablets. From the inscriptions and *cartouches* found there, it is evident that the mines were in full working order at the time of the Exodus, and the neighbourhood of Sarábít el Khádim and of Wády Igné must have been occupied by a large colony of workmen, having most probably a considerable military establishment to preserve discipline amongst them, inasmuch as the miners were chiefly selected from criminals and prisoners of war.

This consideration is a very important one, and may aid us in identifying the true route of the Israelites; for it is most improbable that Moses, well versed as he was in all "the learning of the Egyptians," and acquainted with all the details of their political system, would have led the hosts of Israel into direct contact with those enemies from whom they were then fleeing. Even if the volition of the Lawgiver were not allowed to influence their course, and the miraculous pillar of cloud by day and pillar of fire by night were the people's only guide, yet, as we read in the sacred narrative of no collision with their late taskmasters after the overthrow of Pharaoh and his hosts in the Red Sea, we may fairly conclude that they did not pass by any of those roads which must inevitably have brought them into the very midst of a large Egyptian military settlement. This, therefore, considerably narrows the question by disposing of at least two of the principal routes by which the Israelites could have approached Mount Sinai.

There is another means of access to the ruins of Sarábít el Khádim by a ravine rather higher up the main valley, which involves a less toilsome climb; but as it also necessitates a walk along a narrow sloping ledge of rock, with a terrific precipice beneath, I cannot recommend it to the traveller unless he feels confident in the possession of a sure foot and a steady head.

The name Sarábít el Khádim signifies "the Heights of the Servant," and the place is said by the Arabs to have been so called from a black statue, representing a "servant or slave," which was removed "by the French" during their occupation of Egypt. Amongst the ruins we noticed a pedestal, which might have served for the base of such a statue; and I have since seen in the British Museum a beautifully executed female foot, carved in black stone, which formed part of the collection of curiosities found by the late Major Macdonald in this very spot. It is not unlikely that amidst the antiquities in the Louvre the remaining portion of the "Khádim" from Sarábít may yet be found.

The hieroglyphic inscriptions from Maghárah range from Senefru of the third Egyptian dynasty to Tothmes III. of the 18th line; those of Sarábít el Khádim end with Rameses IV. of the 20th, after which period the mines and temple were abandoned. The date of the Exodus is usually placed by Egyptologists in the reign of Menepthah, son and successor of Rameses II., but others are disposed to place it at the beginning of the 18th dynasty. No inscriptions have been discovered either at Maghárah or Sarábít of kings who reigned between Tothmes III.

and the 12th dynasty, nor any after the 20th. They occur rarely and at long intervals after Rameses II.

One of the principal tablets at Sarábit el Khádim refers to a certain Har-ur-ra, superintendent of the mines, who arrived there in the month Phamenoth, in the reign of some monarch not mentioned, probably of the 12th dynasty. The author of the inscription declares that he never once left the mine; he exhorts the chiefs to go there also and "if your faces fail," says he, "the goddess Athor will give you her arms to aid you in the work. Behold me, how I tarried there after I had left Egypt;—my face sweated, my blood grew hot, I ordered the workmen working daily, and said unto them, there is still turquoise in the mine and the vein will be found in time. And it was so; the vein was found at last and the mine yielded well. When I came to this land, aided by the king's genii, I began to labour strenuously. The troops came and entirely occupied it, so that none escaped therefrom. My face grew not frightened at the work, I toiled cheerfully; I brought abundance, yea abundance of turquoise and obtained yet more by my search. I did not miss a single vein." Another inscription runs: "I came to the mines of my lord, I commenced working the *mafka*, or turquoise, at the rate of 15 men daily. Never was like done in the reign of Senefru the justified..." These and the frequent recurrence of tablets representing the various kings triumphing over and slaying their foreign captives, will enable the reader to judge of the nature of the mines and the manner in which they were worked by their Egyptian discoverers*.

The country around the mines contains numerous evidences of the immense smelting operations carried on by the ancient Egyptians; these could not have been conducted without the consumption of large quantities of timber for fuel, and this gives additional probability to an hypothesis which I have before advanced—that the country was at one time much more plentifully supplied with vegetation, and therefore likely to have had a much more copious rainfall than it has now†.

Having photographed the ruins, and obtained copies or impressions of all the hieroglyphic monuments, we followed our old road until we came to the mouth of Wády Nasb. Here the country begins to get much more open, the sandstone hills be-

---

* For the above information I am indebted to the kindness of Dr S. Birch, of the British Museum, who has read and deciphered the whole of the hieroglyphic inscriptions copied by the Sinai Expedition.

† The following extract from King's "Italian Valleys of the Alps," p. 345, will illustrate these remarks:—

"The specimens (of iron ore) brought to me were very rich and heavy. It has hitherto been worked only in the most clumsy and unscientific manner with the rudest machinery and no tramroads, the ore being chiefly carried from the mines to Aimaville or Villeneuve on the backs of women. Under such circumstances it is hardly to be wondered at, that, as the local supply of wood for fuel began to fail, the rich profit the mines at one time used to yield gradually diminished, until for some years past they have hardly been worked at all."

The destruction of forest by mining is also mentioned, on page 182 of the same work.

coming lower and lower, and less compact in their arrangement. Instead of following the Seil Hamr, by which we had come from Suez, we here turned into a valley called Wády Bab'a, which, though broad, flat and desolate for the first two hours, gradually narrowed and grew more rugged and picturesque as we entered the range of granite mountains through which it finds its way. Finding a pleasant spot, where there was a stream of brackish water and a few palms, we pitched our tent. But we soon saw that we had little reason to congratulate ourselves upon our choice of a camping ground; for no sooner had the shades of night fallen than we were visited by such a plague of insects as it has never been my lot to witness before or since. Mosquitoes, moths and gnats literally swarmed in upon us, extinguishing the candles, filling our ink bottles, settling in large bunches even on the pens with which we wrote, and ultimately driving us out into the dark night-air, to be again charged at by gigantic beetles, and stung by flying ants.

The valley, as we resumed our journey, grew more wild and lonely at every step, contracting at last into a wondrous gorge, where a small stream rushed between steep granite walls, often not more than eight feet apart, and so lofty that the light of day scarce penetrated through the narrow space above into the depths wherein we walked.

At last we emerged from this into a broad open space between cretaceous hills, and after a few more turns and windings came once again in sight of the sea. We were on the plain of El Markhá, a continuation of the wider shore-plain which borders the southwest of the Peninsula; and a dreary, sandy, desolate place it was. The Red Sea lay stretched out mistily before us, a dull haze hiding the horizon line and foreboding some days of sirocco winds and sultry heat. El Markhá, from which the plain is named, is a long white ridge of chalk hills, which run down to the water's edge; the place has only one spring, and that is so brackish as to be quite undrinkable. As there is neither water nor pasturage, the Arabs never come near the spot unless to cross it on their way to and from Suez, and, excepting a few lizards and stray sea-birds, we did not meet with a single living creature on our way.

Keeping along the base of the chalk hills, we made for Wády Taiyebeh, near the mouth of which is a little sandy cape, a flat desolate strip jutting out into the sea; and at the further extremity of this lay the shattered hull of a wrecked vessel. The cape is called Rás Abu Zenímeh, from a *weli*, or saint of that name, who lies buried there. The rude hut which covers his tomb is constructed of the lightest materials, palm-branches and reeds covered with coarse matting; the interior presents a quaint heterogeneous collection of offerings, principally maritime, consisting of every mentionable and unmentionable waif and stray—bits of rag, rope, matting, meat-tins, fish-bones, and lamps; it looked like some ancient marine store which had been transported bodily into the middle of the desert, and there left for ages to rot undisturbed.

The plain at the mouth of Wády Taiyebeh has been suggested as the probable site of the Encampment by the Red Sea; and as, from a comparison of the various routes, we were unanimously of opinion that the Israelites must have taken the lower route by the seashore, we were inclined to acquiesce in this identification.

A short way up the wády, the mountains began to assume a more pleasing and variegated appearance—the sandstone here meeting the chalk hills with a very decided line of demarcation, so that the sides were often half red and half white, and this, relieved by the bright green of many a clustering caper plant, produced an effect extremely agreeable to the eye. Some distance up the valley there is also a scanty *tarfah* grove, and a brackish stream. From Wády Taiyebeh we turned into Wády Etlál, where we camped, and sending the camels on ahead of us in the morning Captain Wilson and I proceeded to explore this valley with a view to ascertaining if there were any practicable road down it to the seashore. However, after an hour's walking, we came into a gorge so narrow and intricate as to be impassable even for foot passengers; it was quite clear, therefore, that the Children of Israel could not have passed that way.

When we had retraced our steps, another hour took us over the intervening plain to Wády Useit, down which we turned again towards the sea. This valley is also so narrow and difficult of passage in certain parts that it would be impossible for a large host to traverse it with their baggage. So that Wády Taiyebeh is the only valley by which the Israelites can have descended to the seashore after crossing Wády Gharandel, supposing them to have taken, as I firmly believe they did, the lower or coast route towards Sinai.

A few hours' walk brought us again to the seashore, where we rejoined Captain Palmer, who had left us at Mukatteb, and while we were engaged at Sarábít el Khádim, had been occupied in surveying in other parts. He had just returned from an excursion to Jebel Bisher, at the base of the mountains of the Tíh, and was encamped by the Hammám Far'ún, or "Pharaoh's Bath." After the fatigues of the day, a bath in this natural hot spring was very acceptable, and we made straight for the spot. A large bluff of white rock comes down almost into the sea, and at the base of this, from several small fissures in the stone, trickles a stream of nearly boiling hot water, which also bubbles up at intervals from the sand. The beach is covered with a white incrustation, and is so hot that one can scarcely stand upon it with naked feet; while a thick sulphurous steam exhales from the sand, making the whole immediate neighbourhood of the springs smell like a medicated vapour bath. A dip at the point where the hot water meets the cool waves is delightful, as the temperature may be graduated at pleasure by moving a few feet either way. Our first bathe was brought to a premature conclusion by the appearance of a huge shark, which suddenly rose within a few feet of where I was standing, and continued to sail gracefully round and round the spot, waiting for a favourable opportunity to snap at the legs of the first person who should venture into the water; we watched his ominous black fin glittering for some time in the light of the setting sun and then turned back to camp. We had to pick our way as best we could in the dark, for so short is the twilight in these regions, that the golden rim had scarcely sunk beneath the horizon when night set in, "and darkness was upon the face of the deep."

The waters of these springs are much resorted to by the Arabs for their medicinal virtues, especially in the case of rheumatic affections, to which the poor Bedawín of Sinai are greatly exposed, owing to the bleak air of their mountains and their insufficient resources of food and raiment. Of course more importance is attached to the superstitious observances with which they accompany their bath than to the efficacy of the waters themselves, and no Arab will venture here to seek relief without bringing an offering to propitiate the angry ghost of Pharaoh, who is supposed to be the presiding genius of the place. This offering generally consists of a cake made up with certain stated proportions of meal, oil, and other ingredients. The following is the Arab legend of the origin of the Hammám Far'ún.

"When our Lord Moses had quarrelled with Pharaoh, and determined to lead the Children of Israel out of Egypt, he found himself stopped by the salt sea, but at the command of God Most High he raised his staff and smote upon the waters, whereupon they parted on the right hand and on the left, and the Children of Israel found a dry passage in the bottom of the deep. Then Pharaoh and his soldiery essayed to follow, but when they had come midway Moses again raised his staff, and, smiting the waters, said, 'Return, O sea, into thy former course,' and the waters closed over the Egyptians, and the Children of Israel saw the corpses of their enemies floating on the waves. But Pharaoh was a mighty man, and struggled with the billows; then, seeing Moses standing on the rock above him, he waxed exceeding wroth, and gave so fierce a gasp that the waters boiled up as they closed over his drowning head. Since that time the angry ghost of the king of Egypt has haunted the deep, and should any unfortunate vessel come near the spot he rises up and overwhelms it in the waves, so that to the present day no ship can sail on Pharaoh's Bath."

The second day of our stay at Hammám Far'ún was one of the hottest we had experienced, the thermometer, even at an early hour in the morning, standing at 95° in the shade. Towards the evening a sudden but violent storm of wind arose, the first gust of which literally tore our tent up from the ground, and buried us without any warning in the *débris.* Captain Palmer, who had ascended the Hammám bluff for the purpose of taking astronomical observations, experienced the full violence of the gale, and did not reach camp until eleven o'clock at night, when he came in bleeding and well-nigh exhausted, having had to scramble down the rugged rocks in the dark without a guide, for the Arabs who accompanied him were too much frightened to venture upon the descent, and preferred passing the night cold and hungry upon the summit. I cannot do better than reproduce here his own narrative of their adventure.

"Jebel Hammám Far'ún," he writes, "gave me one of the hardest nights' climbing I have ever had. I was encamped at its base in the month of March 1869, and had occasion to spend half a night on its summit in order to take some astronomical observations. The ascent in daylight was managed without much difficulty, the weather was calm and clear, and all went on smoothly on the summit. But, hardly had the last observation been completed when there came sweeping down upon us, with a fierce roar, one of the most violent and sudden tempests it has ever been my fate to experience. It broke upon us almost instantaneously, extinguishing our two lamps in a moment, and nearly blowing us, instruments and all, into the sea. So strong was the blast that even mercury, which I was vainly endeavouring to pour from one vessel into another, blew away like spray into the air, and I had the hardest possible work to get all the things secured.

Pharaoh must have been in a terribly angry mood that night, and so the Arabs seemed to think, for, what with the darkness and the tempest, the roaring of the wind, and of the sea 1500 feet below us, the danger of the descent, and their superstitious dread of the whole locality, they were soon reduced to a state of abject terror which was quite ridiculous to witness. One of the four began to bellow, and all except Sálem Ibn Husein, our faithful old guide, implored to be allowed to lie down and die, a permission which was cheerfully accorded. Sálem, I bade follow me, and he did so like a child, and down we blundered in the dark over a crumbling mountain-side, which would have been puzzling enough by day, but on a night so dark and wild as this, was perilous breakneck work. It was three hours before we reached camp, tattered and tired, bruised and bleeding; and now Sálem, who had been praying vigorously all the way down, was almost as noisy with thanksgiving and praise, and poured forth such a tale of our exploits to his comrades in camp as forthwith raised me in their estimation to the rank of a "*jedá*" or athlete. It was no such wonderful achievement after all, though Sálem in his fright seemed to think it so, but it certainly *was* refreshing to show a Bedawí the way over his own wild mountains."

Wishing to push on to Sinai to witness an Arab festival, Captain Wilson and I left the rest of the party to follow by another route, north of Sarbút el Jemel, and hurried on by ourselves along the

Suez road to the convent. At Wády Nasb we made a short détour, to examine the water-spring at the head of that valley, and finding the remains of an excellent ancient road, in all probability constructed by the Egyptians for conveying the ore from the mines in the plateau of Sarábít el Khádim, we crossed over the mountains to Wády Súwig.

On our journey from Suez we had taken the longer route by Wády es Sheikh, but on this occasion we made for the Nagb Hawa, and approached the convent from that direction. The spot had lost nothing of its grandeur in our eyes by contrast with the other scenes amidst which we had passed the last three months, and I still think that the monster avenue of mountains which close in the plain of Er Ráhah with the lone symmetrical peak of the Rás Sufsáfeh at the lower end, stands unrivalled in the desolate beauty of its situation.

We had now examined every possible route into the Peninsula, and had before us all the data that could be obtained for forming an opinion upon the route of the Israelites to the Mount of the Law; it only remained to examine that part of the country which lay between Sinai and the scene of their protracted wanderings before it was permitted them to enter the Promised Land. What was the result of these later investigations, and what were the conclusions at which we arrived upon a *résumé* of our work, I will relate further on.

This chapter has been necessarily deficient in incidents and anecdote, for it is not in these lonely deserts that one meets with amusing adventure; but the earnest student of Sacred History cannot fail to profit by every jot of information, however simply told, which may throw light upon the lands where God was pleased to manifest Himself to man.

CHAPTER XIII.

THE OUTLYING DISTRICTS OF SINAI.

Ascent of Umm Shomer; view from the summit; legend of the Maiden's Rock; mysterious sounds on the mountain. The science of *Gaiyáfeh*. The plain of Sened and Jebel Umm 'Alawí. Copper mines at Jebel Habashí. Trip to 'Ain Hudherah; Erweis el Ebeirig; remains of an Israelitish camp; Kibroth Hattaavah; Hazeroth; Tomb of Nebí Sáleh; ceremonies observed there. Rujeim Zuweidíyeh. Preparations for departure. Wády Tarfah. Night march across el Gáah. Homeward bound.

WE had now to make a tour of the principal outlying mountains and valleys in the Peninsula. The first place to which we bent our steps was Jebel Umm Shomer, whose commanding summit presented a most favourable point for completing the work of triangulation.

Taking the same route over the watershed of Wády Sebáiyeh which we had followed some months before on our way to Jebel Hadíd, we entered a broad, dismal valley called Wády Rahabeh, where a few of the Umm Shomer Arabs had pitched their tents. Seeing us approach, they spread their best carpets by the wayside, and hastened to prepare coffee, of which

they courteously invited us to partake. In deference to the laws of Arabian etiquette, we sat down and chatted with them for some time, and when we rose, to take our departure, the sheikh, to my intense horror, precipitated himself upon my neck and treated me to a stage embrace in token of fraternal amity! When we recall the difficulty which Burckhardt and other earlier travellers experienced from this same tribe, their reception of us affords a striking instance of the change that may be wrought in a people during the lapse of a few years by partial contact with civilisation. A short journey brought us to Wády Zeytúneh, where we pitched our tent in a little garden by a spring of water and a cluster of olive trees. In the morning we made an early start, as the ascent of the mountain is long and tedious. Three lofty ridges have to be crossed before Umm Shomer itself comes in sight: the last of these, Abu Shejer, is 1200 feet above Wády Zeytúneh. The view from the top of Abu Shejer, however, quite repays one for the fatigue and the labour lost in thus ascending ridge after ridge only to come down again nearly to the same level on the other side. Immediately below you lie two valleys; a ridge, crossing from the foot of the mountain on which you stand to some distance up the side of Umm Shomer, forming the watershed between them. That on the right is called Wády Zeraigíyeh, and that on the left hand, Wády Rimhán. Both these wádies contain a goodly quantity of vegetation, including groves of *cárúb*, palm and other trees.

In Wády Zeraigíyeh also stands the ruined convent of Már Antús, now quite dismantled and deserted. In front rises Umm Shomer, a magnificent mass divided into huge jagged peaks, with innumerable chasms and two great ravines running down its sides. On the left the twin peaks of Jebel Rimhán tower majestically into the air, scarcely inferior to Umm Shomer in height or romantic beauty of form, and further still is the huge rounded block of Jebel eth Thebt. There was something even terrible in the desolate seclusion of the silent little convent buried in the heart of this gaunt, stony desert; it seemed the very petrifaction, as it were, of asceticism, soon to rank with other fossil monsters, and tell its tale of extinct superstition and depravity.

Crossing the ridge which divides the two wádies, we reached the point where the actual ascent of Umm Shomer begins. A few minutes' fair walking up the ravine brought us to a shady nook, paved with smooth granite, over which trickled a sparkling stream, its banks being fringed with rushes and clusters of *zárút* or hawthorn trees. As we continued to ascend, the walking became more and more difficult, owing to the treacherous layer of decomposed granite upon which the boulders lie, and which renders one's foothold very insecure. Presently the ravine narrows to a mere crack, and the path has to be picked out amidst great masses of slippery granite, which afford capital exercise for hands as well as feet. At the bottom of this cleft we rested for a few minutes to watch a herd of *bedan*, who looked down upon us from the very summit of the mountain, now peering timidly over some projecting crag, and now bounding on to some isolated pinnacle of rock, and staring with a puzzled inquiring air upon the intruders. The shrill whistle too, which the creature emits when frightened or disturbed, resounded from behind many a stone, betokening the presence of a much larger number than those which we could see. In half an hour more we had reached the foot of the huge granite hemisphere which forms the summit of the highest peak; this has been described by some travellers as so desperate a bit of climbing that we were prepared to find it almost inaccessible. It turned out to be nothing very formidable after all; a good head and practice in stepping over slippery rocks being all that is required for the ascent. Captain Wilson clambered by himself up a fissure on the left, while Captain Palmer and I (unaided by our Arab guides, who predicted broken necks for all three) wriggled up the *cheminée* through which travellers are usually dragged on to the summit; having completed the distance from camp in two hours and twenty-eight minutes. The summit is composed of a number of smooth granite boulders piled together in majestic confusion, the highest point being a round rock which rises about twenty feet above the rest. This structure is the result of the weathering of the rock, and is by no means uncommon in granite districts.

From this we looked down over a sheer precipice of some 3000 feet into the valley beneath; the day was too hazy for a good view of the grand panorama which the position commands, but the fantastic and graceful clouds floating hundreds of feet below us, and the mysterious mountain-shapes seen dimly through the veil of mist, produced a weird effect which in a measure compensated us for the loss of the landscape.

To the south the view was more imposing, comprising the jagged precipitous sides of Umm Shomer's lower peak, with Rimhán, Eth Thebt and other portions of the noble range to back it up. We could just distinguish the little conical peaks of Geráïn 'Utúd in El Gááh, and no doubt, on a clear day, the whole of that extensive wilderness, with the labyrinth of wádies which divide it from the mountain region, might be easily discerned. The Sinai and Serbál groups were also sufficiently well defined for purposes of observation; a vertical angle to Katarína showed a slight elevation, which, added to the correction for curvature of the earth, would make a considerable difference in favour of that peak, thus demolishing the reputation which Umm Shomer has so long enjoyed of being the highest mountain in the Peninsula.

A little way down on the western side of the summit is a projecting rock, cracked in such a manner as almost to suggest that it has been vertically rent and the gap afterwards filled up by the insertion of another stone; it is called by the Arabs Hajar el Bint, or the "Maiden's Rock," and the following legend has attached itself to the spot:—

"Long ages ago, there dwelt upon Umm Shomer a fairy who used to fascinate stray travellers by the exquisite strains which she could elicit from her flute of reeds. She was beautiful beyond mortal loveliness, and her only covering was the long streaming hair which flowed in rich waves over her neck. One day a Bedawí hunter, while pursuing his game in the mountains, came suddenly upon the damsel, who entertained him with pleasant discourse and left him completely enamoured of her charms. In the morning he determined to seek again the mysterious beauty and to bring her back with him by force or stratagem. But, when he came to a point in the road where the path lay through a narrow cleft in the rock, he found that the fairy maiden had anticipated him, and baffled his evil designs by miraculously closing up the fissure in the rock as we behold it at the present day. Since that time she has never again been seen, but gives occasional notice of her presence by firing off a gun (!) one day in every year." The last unromantic and incongruous addition to the legend has been devised by the Arabs to account for certain mysterious sounds which do proceed from the mountain, and which may sometimes be heard as far distant even as the Convent of St Katharine. They are in all probability caused by large masses of rock becoming detached by the action of frost and rolling with a mighty crash over the precipice into the valley below. We noticed on the summit several places in which masses of rock had been recently disengaged in this manner, and all the higher portions of the surrounding mountains exhibit traces of a similar phenomenon. Most previous travellers have applied to the whole summit the name of Hajar el Bint, and seem to have been unaware both of the legend and of the real position of the stone.

In coming down we selected the fissure by which Wilson had gained the top; and, when I remember the places over which we passed, I should be inclined to reverse the judgment of a justly celebrated mountaineer (who was, however, prevented by illness from himself ascending the mountain), and say that the ascent of Umm Shomer is not very severe but is in places rather dangerous.

When we reached the summit, the air was so still and calm that a lighted match burnt steadily upon the highest point. As we came down, a few drops of rain fell, a fresh wind sprang up, and by the time we had returned to camp a hurricane was blowing which threatened every moment to bring the tent about our ears. We were of course ravenously hungry after the fatigues of the day, and 'Eisa our servant, having kept us waiting, was sternly rebuked for his negligence; he was so demoralised however by the wind and rain as to venture to make a retort; whereupon the following dialogue took place:—

CAPTAIN PALMER (*with withering sarcasm*). "I suppose when you get back to Suez you'll want a character?"

'EISA (*bewildered and disorganised*). "Curry-powder sar? no sar, got plenty."

Next day, we started for Wády Wáará, to excavate at the *nawámis* or stone remains near its head which we had left untouched on our previous visit to this neighbourhood. On our way we had an experience of the use and application of those Arab tribe-marks which one finds in such profusion in many parts of the desert, and which have been more than once described as "ancient astronomical signs." Old Sálem was the only member of the party who knew the road, and fearing that the men with the baggage-camels, who were some distance behind us, might lose the way, especially as we were turning out of the main valley up a narrow and insignificant glen, he undertook to give them notice of the road which we had taken. Drawing a line (called *jurreh*) across the mouth of the side valley to attract their attention, he traced the mark of his own tribe, the Jibalíyeh, and that of the camel-drivers, the Auláe Sa'íd, with his finger on the sand, and set above this the print of his naked foot with the toes pointing in the direction we were about to take. After this we proceeded on our way without anxiety, and our camel-men followed us as surely as if they had been conducted by a skilful guide. The science of *gaiyáfeh*, or "following on the trail," has always been a favourite one with the Arabs, who, while often utterly unobservant of surrounding objects and entirely indifferent to the charms of scenery, will rarely allow the slightest object on the ground to escape their notice. Wonderful stories are told of the skill thus displayed, and Bedawín authorities assert that in the Belád er Raml, "the sandy district" to the east of Idumæa, there are tribes so astute that, were a man to come by night to one of their palm-groves, eat a single date, and escape without having been seen by a living soul, yet, if he were to return to the same spot after years of absence, he would be instantly recognised and charged with the theft! Allowing for Oriental exaggeration, it is certain that the Arabs do possess a remarkable instinct for the recognition of footprints; and our own guides have often pointed out to me the tracks of their friends, and even indicated the time which had elapsed since they had passed, and that amongst a confusion of the tracks of camels, goats and men.

The *nawámis* at Wády Waárá are burial-places of the "stone-circle" class. One of them which I opened consisted of a ring of upright stones about three feet in height, with a smaller ellipse in the centre. Inside this was the cist in which the actual interment had been made; it was covered with such heavy boulders that, even with the assistance of four Arabs, I had great difficulty in removing them. The skeleton was lying in a doubled-up position, and accompanied by a few shells and worked flints.

Crossing Wádies Nasb and Rutig, with which the reader is already familiar, we entered the mountain chain which forms the eastern wall of Wády Seba'íyeh. Our road lay up Wády Melezz, at the head of which we came across a collection of *nawámis* consisting of upright stones, some arranged in circles connected by passages, and others forming an enclosure nearly fifty feet square. They would seem to belong to some ancient system of hill fortification. Passing over one or two watersheds, we at length emerged into the plain of Es Sened. With all our experience of the country, we were scarcely prepared for the magnificent prospect which here opened out before us.

Es Sened is an extensive plain dotted here and there with bare and curiously weathered rocks which serve to show off its vast proportions to better advantage; on the south-eastern side rises Jebel Umm 'Alawí, a fine rugged crag of red granite, with lower mountains falling away on either side and forming a huge crescent or amphitheatre. At the opposite side the country is more open, and a magnificent view is obtained of the Tíh range beyond the low rugged hills which bound the plain.

It is a curious circumstance that such a remarkable feature in the Peninsula should have remained so long unknown, for, until visited by Mr Holland a year or two before, its existence had not even been heard of. We could not help feeling struck with the remarkable fitness of this spot in every feature to the requirements of the sacred narrative of the Giving of the Law; but considerations of the route and the entire absence of any tradition in its favour forbade us to indulge in the dream, or to waver in our allegiance to the Sinai of Er Ráhah.

Leaving Captain Palmer to survey Es Sened and

the neighbouring districts, Captain Wilson and I started off on an excursion to 'Ain Hudherah, which has been identified on account of both its name and position with the Hazeroth of the Bible. On our way we stayed to examine the copper mines, discovered by Mr Holland, near Jebel Habashí on the northern outskirts of the plain. They are situated in a wády called Regaitá, where a large dyke runs through the granite, along the top of a low ridge of hills, and contains thin veins of the metal in a very pure form. The grain of the rock itself also contains a considerable quantity of the ore in minute particles, but the miners appear to have been ignorant of any method for crushing the stone, and seem to have contented themselves with picking out the thin layers of sulphate of copper from the dyke. At the end of the ridge the ore has been worked out in a small cave, and in one place, where the vein takes a dip, a shaft has been sunk to a considerable depth. As we had no ropes with us, we could not properly explore this shaft, which we much regretted, because the rock here appears to have been extensively undermined. The neighbouring hills are covered with pathways in every direction, and the numerous remains of smelting furnaces which may still be seen, show that mining operations were once carried on upon a very large scale in the vicinity. They were doubtless Egyptian, but the rude method of working, and the absence of any hieroglyphic or other inscriptions, would point to an antiquity far greater than that of Maghárah or Sarábít.

The road from this point is featureless and uninteresting, crossing a succession of barren plains for some hours, and ultimately falling into the Wády Saá'l, the ordinary route of travellers from the Convent to 'Akabah. While passing through this wády, we came upon a herd of *bedan*, which trotted across the path in front of our camels, and were soon lost to sight in a deep ravine on the opposite side of the valley. A stately long-bearded patriarch with magnificent horns led the van, the females with young ones trotting by their side followed, and the ablebodied males brought up the rear. After a few hours, this valley widens out almost into a plain, and contains a great quantity of thorny acacias; one magnificent *Talha* amongst the number being by far the largest tree in Sinai, and affording a most grateful shade from the midday heat.

A little further on, and upon the watershed of Wády el Hebeibeh, we came to some remains which, although they had hitherto escaped even a passing notice from previous travellers, proved to be among the most interesting in the country. The piece of elevated ground which forms this watershed is called by the Arabs Erweis el Ebeirig, and is covered with small enclosures of stones. These are evidently the remains of a large encampment, but they differ essentially in their arrangement from any others which I have seen in Sinai or elsewhere in Arabia; and on the summit of a small hill on the right is an erection of rough stones surmounted by a conspicuous white block of pyramidal shape. The remains extend for miles around, and, on examining them more carefully during a second visit to the Peninsula with Mr Drake, we found our first impression fully confirmed, and collected abundant proofs that it was in reality a deserted camp. The small stones which formerly served, as they do in the present day, for hearths, in many places still showed signs of the action of fire, and on digging beneath the surface we found pieces of charcoal in great abundance. Here and there were larger enclosures marking the encampment of some person more important than the rest, and just outside the camp were a number of stone heaps, which, from their shape and position, could be nothing else but graves. The site is a most commanding one, and admirably suited for the assembling of a large concourse of people.

Arab tradition declares these curious remains to be "the relics of a large Pilgrim or Hajj caravan, who in remote ages pitched their tents at this spot on their way to 'Ain Hudherah, and who were soon afterwards lost in the desert of the Tîh, and never heard of again."

For various reasons I am inclined to believe that this legend is authentic, that it refers to the Israelites, and that we have in the scattered stones of Erweis el Ebeirig real traces of the Exodus.

Firstly: they are said *táhu*, to have "lost their way," the Arabic verb from which the name *Tîh*, or "Wilderness of the Wanderings," is derived. Secondly: they are described as a Hajj caravan; at the first glance this would seem an anachronism, as the word is employed exclusively by the Muslims, and applied to their own annual pilgrimage to Mecca. But this very term owes its origin to the Hebrew *Hagg*, which signifies "a festival," and is the identical word used in Exodus (x, 9) to express the ceremony which the Children of Israel alleged as their reason for wishing to leave Egypt—namely: "to hold *a feast* unto the Lord" in the wilderness. It could not apply to the modern Mohammedan Hajj Caravan, for that has never passed this way, and would not under any circumstances find it necessary to go to 'Ain Hudherah; but the Children of Israel did journey to Hazeroth, and the tradition is therefore valuable in determining the latter site as well as their subsequent route on leaving the Peninsula. The length of time which has elapsed since the events of the Exodus furnishes no argument against the probability of this conclusion, for there are other monuments in the country in even better preservation, and of a date indisputably far anterior. It is a curious fact that, if you ask twenty different Arabs to relate to you one of their national legends, they will all do so in precisely the same words, thus showing with what wonderful precision oral tradition is handed down from generation to generation among them.

These considerations, the distance—exactly a day's journey—from 'Ain Hudherah, and those mysterious graves outside the camp, to my mind prove conclusively the identity of this spot with the scene of that awful plague by which the Lord punished the greed and discontent of His people; where "the wrath of the Lord was kindled against the people, and the Lord smote the people with a very great plague. And he called the name of that place Kibroth-Hattaavah; *because there they buried the people that lusted.* And the people journeyed from Kibroth-Hattaavah unto Hazeroth, and abode at Hazeroth." (Numbers xi. 33, 34, 35.)

And we journeyed on in their track, passing over desolate sandy plains dotted with weird sandstone crags, until we reached 'Ain Hudherah. Although this place is mentioned as a station in the ordinary road to 'Akabah, no European except Mr Holland and ourselves appears ever to have visited it before.

Travellers usually stay to rest at a large isolated rock, in the centre of the plain, called Hudheibat Hajjáj, "The hill of the Hajj pilgrims" (again reminding us of those first Hajjis who may have also enjoyed "the shadow of this great rock in a weary land"), while their Arabs, who take water at 'Ain Hudherah, descend to it from Wády el Ghazáleh, an hour or two on the other side. But, did the pilgrim know that the uninviting cleft in the white limestone rock some half an hour further on, and not ten minutes from his camel track, looked down on Hazeroth, he would turn aside and gaze upon what is without exception the most beautiful and romantic landscape in the Desert. Advancing towards the cleft, as we did at the close of the day, all was bare, barren and desolate; and a violent sand-storm, obscuring the mountains to the southwest, made the

prospect drearier still. Great and pleasant then was our surprise when, on reaching the cliff, we gazed for the first time on 'Ain Hudherah.

Through a steep and rugged gorge, with almost perpendicular sides, we looked down upon a wády-bed that winds along between fantastic sandstone rocks, now rising in the semblance of mighty walls or terraced palaces, now jutting out in pointed ridges—rocky promontories in a sandy sea. Beyond this lies a perfect forest of mountain peaks and chains, and on their left a broad white wády leads up towards the distant mountains of the Tíh. But the great charm of the landscape lies in its rich and varied colouring; the sandstone, save where some great block has fallen away and displayed the dazzling whiteness of the stone beneath, is weathered to a dull red or violet hue, through which run streaks of the brightest yellow and scarlet mixed with rich dark purple tints. Here and there a hill or dyke of green-stone, or a rock of rosy granite, contrasts or blends harmoniously with the rest; and in the midst, beneath a lofty cliff, nestles the dark green palm-grove of Hazeroth. This picture, framed in the jagged cleft, and lit up by the evening sun, with the varied tints and shades upon its mountain background, and the awful stillness that might be seen as Egypt's darkness could be felt, was such a landscape as none but the Great Artist's hand could have designed.

Before leaving, we made a complete examination of the place. The fountain itself rises in the rock behind the palm-grove, and is conducted, by an aqueduct cut in the solid granite, into a reservoir or pool, from which it is let out by a rude sluice to irrigate the gardens which the Arabs still cultivate here. The remains of several well-constructed walls point to a former and perhaps Christian occupation of the place. The present owners, two members of the Emzeineh tribe, took us to see a large crack in the flat surface of the rock behind the spring and called the Báb er Rúm or "Christian's gate." They say that the ancient inhabitants opened a door in the mountain and constructed a passage through it to their own country Rúm (or Asia Minor), and, having built a city within the subterranean depths and conveyed thither an incalculable treasure, they closed it up after them by the same magical arts which had enabled them to effect an entry.

We returned by the road which we had taken from Es Sened, turning off however to the convent by the spring of Abu Suweirah, and striking Wády es Sheikh just by the tomb of Nebí Sáleh. This tomb consists of two small buildings; the first, a square hovel without a door, is called the *'Arisheh*, and is the place in which the Arabs assemble to perform the preliminary ceremonies before the annual festival which takes place there; the other is a round building, somewhat like a primitive mosque, having a *mihráb* or arched recess in the wall to indicate the Kibleh or direction of the Kaábeh at Mecca. This contains the cenotaph of the sheikh, which is made after the fashion of ordinary Muslim tombs, and is covered with a *Kisweh* of white linen, a tattered green cloth being thrown over the head to represent the green turban worn as a distinctive badge by the companions and descendants of the Prophet. Over the cenotaph are arranged some rough poles in the form of a sloping roof; from which depend the simple offerings of devotees, chiefly pieces of coloured rag. On the ground lay a cross made of two sticks tied together and ornamented with strips of red and white cloth. While we were inspecting the spot, Hammád, one of our camel-men, entered the building, and having first recited the Fátihah or opening chapter of the Corän, and made a prostration before the mihráb, took up a handful of dust from the tomb, which he sprinkled, as he went out, upon his own head and that of his camel. The head of the tomb is turned towards the east; we saw no blood upon the door-posts, or on the tomb itself, as is usual in desert *welis*, but the reason assigned for this by the Arabs was that on the occasion of sacrifice they place two stones by the door to receive the blood, and that these are afterwards removed in order that the tomb may be kept pure and clean. The festival which takes place at the tomb of Nebí Sáleh is considered as the great national event of the year, and the Towarah come from all quarters of the Peninsula, accompanied by their wives and families, to take part in it. On the appointed day, all flock to the spot, dressed in their best attire, the women mounted upon gaily caparisoned dromedaries, while the men, leading their beasts, keep up a lively fire of compliments and repartees. In the immediate vicinity of the saint's tomb a large tent is erected, to serve as a place of public assembly; and the private camps are ranged around. When all is prepared, dromedary races take place, the women encouraging the competitors by the shrill *zaghárit*. The whole company then makes the circuit of the tomb, after which the sheep to be sacrificed are brought up to the door, their ears are cut, and the blood which issues from the wound sprinkled on the posterns. The men next adjourn to the tents, kill and dress the sheep, and prepare their meal. Those who have slaughtered an animal bring the meat in large bowls, and a master of the feast is appointed, who dispenses it to the assembled guests; the portions are handed round in order, according to the position or claims of the recipient. When the meal, followed by the inevitable coffee and pipes, is at an end, each of the party takes a ready trimmed lamp, and goes off to the tomb; there he lights it, burns incense, and, having recited the Fátihah, takes up a little dust from the tomb and sprinkles it upon the heads of his sheep, camels, &c., by way of invoking upon them a blessing from the saint. When this ceremony is over, the women and girls also visit the tomb in parties of six or seven, and are usually followed by the young men of the tribe, who remain with them joking and laughing until a late hour; the evening concludes with the *Mesámereh*, a performance which I have already described. The strictest decorum, however, is always maintained on these occasions. Twenty-four minutes' walk past the tomb of Nebí Sáleh, on the road to Jebel Músa, are some cairns of white stones on the hill-side to the left; these are called Rujeim Zuweidíyeh, and are said to have been placed there by Abu Zeid, the great national hero of Arabia, to commemorate a victory obtained by him over the Barbarians. This tradition gives greater probability to the hypothesis, which I have before advanced, that Sinai was peopled formerly by other than a pure Arab race, and that the present Bedawín "came over with the (Mohammedan) Conquest."

Our few remaining days at the convent were spent in preparations for our departure. It was not without emotion that we bade adieu to the freedom of desert life, and contemplated exchanging our careless roving habits for the conventionalities and proprieties of the civilised world. The vacant, jovial countenances of the monks were clouded by something of a human regret as we bade them adieu, and the poor Bedawín who had been so long dependent on us for employment and bread exhibited a sorrow that even *bakhshísh* could not dispel.

Before leaving, we induced some of the brethren to sit for their portraits to Sergeant Macdonald. The results are not satisfactory; for, although as photographs they are faultless, they fail to render that picturesque squalor which is so typical of the gang. This is no doubt owing to their having performed, on this occasion only, the astoundingly intrepid action of washing their faces. I fear that, if another such event were to occur, rheumatism would decimate the convent of St Katharine. At last we mounted our dromedaries, rode up the valley, took a last look at the convent, and disappeared over the Moneijáh pass. Old Sálem watched us out of sight; he evidently wished to explode, as he had done on the occasion of Holland's departure, but, "strangers being present," he contented himself with a series of ghastly grins and chewing a piece of stick. Wády Seba'íyeh, Engaib 'Imrán or "Amram's pass," and Wády Rahabeh were to us old ground, but presently we entered the Thilmeh or pass of Wády Tarfah. The road was very bad, lying over loose boulders, which are made additionally insecure by a stream of running water that trickles over them; one of our camels slipped, and injured its shoulder so severely that its load had to be taken off and distributed amongst the other beasts. On arriving at a sufficiently spacious place, we halted for the night, but were up and in the saddle before sunrise on the following morning. The start was attended by an ill-omened circumstance, for we had scarcely got under weigh, before a crow, intent on plunder and ticks, settled on the back of one of the camels, and, the intelligent beast taking fright thereat, a general stampede occurred, which threatened our instruments and photographs with immediate destruction. As we neared Jebel Rimhán, the road became nearly impassable, and many of the camels fell upon the wet slippery rocks; thanks however to the quiet and attentive conduct of Sheikh Hassan and his men, the loads were rescued without any serious damage. After this point the valley became more picturesque than before, and the numerous gigantic boulders, some more than a hundred feet high, which are here and there lodged in the wády-bed, tell plainly of the fearful and violent storms which sometimes sweep over this region. On the extreme summit of a conical crag, about 1500 feet above us, we noticed a curious rock, measuring from a hundred to a hundred and fifty feet in height by sixty in breadth, which is balanced like a cromlech upon a mere point of stone; it looked as though one heave with a crowbar would roll it over into the valley beneath.

Presently the scene changed from one of utter devastation and a wilderness of scattered boulders, to a narrow gorge, with immensely high and perpendicular walls of rock, resembling Wády Babá, but on a larger scale. This is the pass over the range of Jebel eth Thebt, and from it we emerged into a fair open valley leading out upon the plain of El Gáah. We reached the plain about 5 o'clock P.M., and having partaken of a frugal meal and slept for two hours as only desert travellers can sleep at a moment's notice, we prepared for a midnight ride across the plain.

It was a sight to be remembered in after years, that long and picturesque caravan trailing across the sand beneath the light of the silvery moon, more like some ghostly cortège of the ancient eastern world than modern travellers of this age of telegraphs and steam. The Arabs wrapped in their flowing robes, the huge camels striding along with measured, noiseless tread, the deep shadows, and, above all, the faint cloud-like outline of the mountain mass behind us, increased the illusion, and we marched along slowly and silently, as though we feared that a spoken word would break the spell and cause the mysterious and romantic scene to vanish away.

Just as the moon sunk down, we entered the palm-grove of Tor, and, making for the seashore, awaited the morning light amidst the broken timbers and shattered hulks that lined the beach. A small government transport steamer had been sent to convey us to Suez, and in a few hours we had left the desert, and the work of the Sinai Expedition was over.

CHAPTER XIV.

THE RESULTS OF THE SINAI EXPEDITION.

Bearings upon the history of the Exodus. Authority for identifying the country surveyed with the Sinai of the Bible. Route of the Israelites from Egypt and Sinai. *Résumé* of Arguments. Conclusion.

VIEWED merely as a contribution to geographical science, the accurate investigation of a country so little known as Sinai is undoubtedly a valuable work. But the chief interest of the Peninsula must always lie in its connexion with the Bible Narrative; and it is only in so far as they elucidate or illustrate Holy Scripture that we can judge of, or appreciate, the results obtained by the Sinai Expedition. I have endeavoured, by portraying the country as it is, to enable the reader to form his own opinions upon this subject, but it may be not inappropriate here to mention briefly the conclusions at which we have ourselves arrived, and to point out how the various facts which we have brought to light bear upon the history of the Exodus.

The matter resolves itself into this: A circumstantial account is given in the Bible of an event so important that upon our acceptance or rejection of it as an historical fact depends the whole question of our religious belief,—of the truth or falsehood of the Old Testament. Such a position could not long remain unassailed, and we are accordingly met with numberless objections, which nothing but actual knowledge of the country can enable us to discuss, much less to answer.

I shall deal with the question as purely one of evidence, taking the plain unvarnished statements of the history, and comparing them one by one with the present topographical facts.

It may well be asked, what authority have we for assuming that the Peninsula now known by the name of Sinai is that in which the Mountain of the Law is situated; or that the Passage of the Red Sea took place at the head of the Gulf of Suez, rather than at the Gulf of 'Akabah?

The itinerary in Numbers xxxiii. supplies us with a conclusive answer. The Children of Israel reached the seacoast in three days after leaving Rameses, and no possible theory of the position of that town could bring it within three days' journey of the Gulf of 'Akabah. The Gulf of Suez is, however, distant exactly three days' journey from the site of Memphis, in which neighbourhood at least the ancient capital of Egypt must have stood, and it is therefore certain that the Gulf of Suez is the Red Sea referred to in the history. The same authority tells us that the

Children of Israel did not take the northern road to Palestine by way of Gaza, so that there is absolutely no other course which they could have taken, after crossing to the Asiatic coast, than the road which lies between the steep wall-like escarpment of Jebel er Ráhah and the Red Sea.

This would conduct them towards the mountainous district in the centre of the Peninsula, and it is consequently evident that we are so far right in looking for Mount Sinai in that region. Having satisfied ourselves that we are upon the track of the Israelites, we have next to determine the route which they must have taken. In many countries it would be impossible to pitch upon one road to the exclusion of all the rest, but, thanks to the peculiar nature of the country under consideration, we are enabled, by an exhaustive process, if not to prove, at least to arrive at a more than plausible conjecture upon, this point.

The Israelites were travelling in heavy marching order, taking with them their wives, children, household effects, and indeed all their worldly possessions. We learn that they even had waggons with them during their journey, for we are told, in Numbers vii. 3, that "the Princes of Israel brought their offering before the Lord, six covered waggons and twelve oxen."

Under these circumstances, difficult or intricate passes and defiles are out of the question, and our attention is confined to those roads which are passable for a large caravan with heavily laden beasts of burden.

It may be objected that, as the Israelite host was miraculously guided "by the Pillar of Cloud by day, and the Pillar of Fire by night," we need not, or ought not, to argue from the probabilities suggested by the physical features of the country. To this I would answer that we are expressly told that "God went before them by day in a pillar of cloud *to lead them the way*," not to make for them a road, but to guide them in the best and easiest path, and we are therefore the more bound to take into consideration everything which could give one road preference over another.

The difficulty of providing water for the cattle by which they were accompanied has proved a great stumbling-block to many, but this Mr Holland has considerably lessened by a novel and ingenious suggestion. He believes that, instead of being an encumbrance to the movements of the host, they were used as beasts of burden, and that, in addition to the camp-furniture, each carried its own supply of water, sufficient for several days, in water-skins slung at its sides, precisely as Sir Samuel Baker found them doing at the present day in Abyssinia*.

The spot bearing the name of 'Ayún Músa, Moses' Wells, is no doubt traditionally connected with the Exodus, and was very probably the first camping-place of the Israelites after crossing the Red Sea. From this point the road is unmistakeable for the first three days, since it lies over a flat strip of desert, across which they would naturally choose the

* Paper read before the Church Congress, 1869.

straightest and most direct path. The Bible dismisses this part of their journey in a few words: "they went out into the wilderness of Shur; and "they went three days in the wilderness, and found "no water." (Exodus xv, 22); but I doubt if a more suggestive description could possibly be given of this monotonous waterless waste, the only impressive feature of which is the long *shur*, or "wall," which forms its northern limit.

The next verse proceeds, "and when they came "to Marah, they could not drink of the waters of "Marah, for they were bitter." Now the soil throughout this part of the country, being strongly impregnated with *natrûn*, produces none but bitter or brackish water; and it is worth observing, that the first of these springs with which we meet, 'Ain Hawwárah, is reached on the third day of our desert journey to Sinai.

They next "came to Elim, where were twelve wells of water, and three score and ten palm-trees." Here again, our own experience accords with that of the Israelites, for our next station is in Wády Gharandel, which contains a considerable amount of vegetation, palm-trees in great numbers among the rest, and a perennial stream. It would be of course idle to contend that this is the identical oasis mentioned in Exodus, but I would remind the reader that a supply of water larger than usual, and a consequently larger proportion of vegetation, depends upon the geological configuration of the country, and that, although individual springs may disappear, and break forth again at other places in the vicinity, a few thousand years are not likely to make any very radical change in this respect. Whole districts may be, and often are, rendered barren and dry by the diminution of the rainfall, consequent upon neglect and the destruction of vegetation; but, where a spot like Gharandel still exists, in spite of the deteriorating influences which have been at work in Sinai, we may fairly assume that its fertility dates from a very remote period of antiquity.

"And they removed from Elim, and encamped by the Red Sea," (Num. xxxiii, 10). To reach the sea, two roads were open to them,—either to follow Wády Gharandel itself to its mouth, or to turn down the next practicable valley, Wády Taiyebeh. The first is extremely unlikely, as the cliffs and rough rocks which come down to the water's edge past this point would have impeded their further progress, and compelled them to retrace their steps; whereas from Wády Taiyebeh the coast is open and passable, and moreover the mouth of the valley affords a fine clear space for their encampment by the sea. There are two roads to Sinai, the upper one by Sarábít el Khádim, and the lower one by the coast; and the modern traveller who chooses the latter still turns off by Wády Taiyebeh, and reaches the sea-shore in a fair day's journey from Gharandel. There are several reasons which would have led to the selection of this route by the Israelite hosts; the rugged passes and narrow valleys on the upper road would have presented insuperable difficulties to a large caravan encumbered by heavy baggage, and they would have passed through a district actually held by a large military force of the very enemies from whom they were fleeing. The Bible, however, speaks of no collision between the Egyptians and Israelites, during the whole of their wanderings, after the passage of the Red Sea. Between Wády Gharandel and Wády Taiyebeh, two valleys, Wády Useit and Wády Ethál, descend to the sea; but the first of these is precluded as a route to Sinai for the same reason that leads us to reject Wády Gharandel, viz. that the cliffs of Jebel Hammám Far'ún, a short way south of its mouth, cut off progress along shore; and the second becomes impassable, even for pedestrians, towards its mouth: so that we are forced to the conclusion that Wády Taiyebeh was the only road down which the Children of Israel could have marched.

On the supposition that they did so, the wilderness of Sin will be the narrow strip of desert which fringes the coast south of Wády Taiyebeh; and although it is impossible to define with exactness the next two stations, Dophkah and Alush, we may fairly presume that they lay within the next two days' journey, which would bring the Israelites well into Wády Feirán. Travellers by this route in the present day do not follow Wády Feirán, but turn off by Wády Shellál, and make for Wády Mukatteb by the Nagb Buderah, but the road over that pass was unquestionably constructed at a date posterior to the Exodus, and, had it even existed at that time, would have been less practicable than Wády Feirán, and would not only have led the Israelites into collision with the Egyptians at Maghárah, but have presented a further difficulty in the pass of Jebel Mukatteb. Beyond Wády Feirán there is no practicable valley: Wády Hebrán, the most open of them all, being far too difficult and rugged to have admitted of their passing through it. I have already discussed the reasons both legendary and geographical for placing Rephidim at Hesy el Khattátín in Wády Feirán, and if we read the verse, Exodus xix, 12, "and they departed from Rephidim, and pitched in the wilderness of Sinai," as implying a break in the march between Rephidim and the Mount of the Law (as was suggested on page 161), we shall find that the natural route from Egypt to Sinai accords exactly with the simple and concise account given in the Bible of the Exodus of the Chosen People.

In these conclusions all the members of the Expedition are agreed. Mr Holland, it is true, dissents upon one point, the position of Rephidim, which he would place at El Watíyeh, believing that the whole host of the Israelites turned off from Wády Feirán up Wády es Sheikh, and that the battle with the Amalekites took place long after Feirán had been passed. In the main facts of the route, however, and in the identification of Jebel Músa with Mount Sinai, our investigations have led us to form one unanimous opinion.

We are thus able not only to trace out a route by which the Children of Israel could have journeyed, but also to show its identity with that so concisely but graphically laid down in the Pentateuch. We have seen, moreover, that it leads to a mountain answering in every respect to the description of the Mountain of the Law; the chain of topographical evidence is complete, and the maps and sections may henceforth be confidently left to tell their own tale.

The arguments against objections founded on the supposed incapability of the Peninsula to have supported so large a host, I need not recapitulate here; in the evidence adduced of the greater fertility which once existed in Sinai, and in the actual measurements of its areas, the reader has all the data for himself to decide upon these points.

We cannot perhaps assign much importance to Arab traditions relating to the Exodus as an argument for or against, the truth of the story, but it is at least interesting to know that such traditions are found, and it is satisfactory to have them in a collected and accessible form. Such legends, as we might expect, are chiefly attached to particular localities; they do not follow the Children of Israel by any single or consistent route through the Peninsula, but any spot possessing peculiar features, wherever it may be situated, is connected by the simple Arab with the grand, mysterious figure of the Hebrew prophet, whose memory still lingers in the wild traditions of Sinai.

Such spots are, (1) Moses' wells at 'Ayún Músa near Suez, and 'Ain Músa on Jebel Músa. (2) Moses' seats: at Abu Zeníineh, on the sea-shore near Hammám Far'ún, is shown the place where Moses watched the drowning of the Egyptians, and in the pass of El Watíyeh the chair-shaped rock, now called Magâd en Nebí, is supposed to have received its peculiar shape from the impress of the prophet's form. Similar rocks are found in the valley (Wády ed Deir) in which the convent of St Katharine is situated, and upon the summit of Jebel Músa itself. (3) Rocks struck by Moses; that in Wády Berráh supposed to have been cleft in twain by Moses' sword; the Hajjar el Magarín in the path along Wády Lejá, and Hesy el Khattátín in Wády Feirán. The Hajjar Músa in the vicinity of the convent, which is pointed out to pilgrims as the true rock in Horeb, is a palpable fiction of the monks, and is virtually disregarded by the Arabs. 4. Moses' Baths; as the Hammám Syedná Músa at Tor. The Bedawí version of the passage of the Red Sea, and the legend of the building of stone huts (*nawámis*) by the Children of Israel to keep off the plague of mosquitoes, I have already given. Enough has been said to prove that the inhabitants of the country are themselves thoroughly imbued with the idea that their own desolate and rocky land was once the scene of a great and wonderful manifestation of God to man.

The Mohammedan tradition, as elsewhere current also, evidently points to Jebel Músa as the true Mount Sinai. The description given by the commentators on the Corân of the "Holy wâdy of Towa" where Moses halted amidst the snow and mist, could scarcely apply to any other spot, while the distance, according to the same authority, of Midian from Egypt, exactly tallies with the position of Feirân. Whether, therefore, we look at the results obtained in physical geography alone, or take into consideration the mass of facts which the traditions and nomenclature disclose, we are bound to admit that the investigations of the Sinai Expedition do materially confirm and elucidate the history of the Exodus.

The sojourn of the Children of Israel in Sinai occupies but a comparatively small portion of the long and weary years during which they were condemned to wander in the wilderness, but the thrilling interest of the events which there took place, events not only of paramount influence upon the history of the Jews themselves, but even upon the religious history of Humanity, must always give to this little peninsula a greater share of importance in our eyes. Still our task would be incomplete if we failed to follow up the clue, and trace the Chosen People through all their wanderings until they reached the Promised Land. We have seen how, in the case of Sinai, physical facts accord with the inspired account, and it now remains for us to examine the extensive tract of desert further north, and there to test again the accuracy of Scripture details. It has fallen to my lot to pursue these investigations in many a remote and barren spot of which geography could give no account, and as my second journey was undertaken at a different time and under different circumstances to that which I have hitherto described, I shall narrate my subsequent experiences in another series of chapters.

www.ingramcontent.com/pod-product-compliance
Lightning Source LLC
Chambersburg PA
CBHW030749230426
43667CB00007B/904